mindful
ness
torah&
redemp
tion

thirtysix.org

Mindfulness, Torah & Redemption

The Mindful Approach to Personal & National Redemption

ISBN 9798618747639

Published by:
Thirtysix.org
22 Yitzchak Road
Telzstone, Kiryat Yearim
Israel   90838

Those who *mindfully* helped
with the publication
of this book.

Sammy Goldfinger

Chaim Bitton

Felix Gruman

Sandy Shields

Rivka Zahavy

Akiva Abrams

Your body is present How about your mind?

ON A RECENT trip to the United States a book cover caught my eye in an airport store. The paperback had a white cover with only "mindfulness" written on it in block letters. It was simple but elegant, and I picked it up for a quick glance because I had thought of doing something similar with a future book of my own.

I decided to buy it, however, because the topic of mindfulness has interested me for some time now. I'm always curious about ways to expand mental capacity and improve the quality of life. From the cover, it seemed to be something that could help with this.

I began reading the book on the plane, but was

quickly disappointed to find that there wasn't much new for me. After pointing out that "mindfulness" is a buzzword today, the author explained in detail how it has been used to greatly increase productivity in the workplace and life in general. Much of the information I already knew or just found obvious, so after skimming through the rest of the book, I put it away.

Then it occurred to me: the reason so much of the material was familiar was because my life was already based on mindfulness. It's built into me from the moment I wake up in the morning, start each day with "*Modeh ani lefanecha…*,"[1] and go to sleep at the end of the day after *Krias Shema al HaMittah*.[2]

Then there are the myriad *mitzvos* that I get to perform in between those two times. I'll doven three times a day and make a *brochah* after using the bathroom several times. I'll have three meals and a few snacks, and they all will require blessings before and after.

All those *mitzvos* take place against a backdrop of the six constant *mitzvos*—including love and fear of God—which are incumbent on all Jews every waking moment of their lives. The *mitzvos* are supposed to

---

[1] Traditionally said upon waking, it means "I give thanks before you, King, living and eternal, for You have returned within me my soul with compassion; abundant is Your faithfulness!"

[2] The prayers recited before going to sleep.

inspire me to act my godliest at every moment, to make sure that when I do *mitzvos*, I am MINDFUL of them and what they need from me to do their job.

Of course there is always the danger of performing *mitzvos* mindLESSly, what is called "by rote." People know they have an obligation, and they wouldn't consider not performing it. They just don't think about what they are doing while doing it, but are rather on autopilot instead.

The number one problem? Distraction. We're easily distracted, and life is very distracting. There's always something going on around people to pull their attention away from the *mitzvah* at hand, especially at the last minute. Dovid *HaMelech* died only because he became distracted from his learning just long enough to fall and fatally hurt himself.[3]

In fact Amalek's[4] chief method of attacking a Jew is with distraction. When we left Egypt, Amalek attacked us as a nation.[5] Since then its reality has attacked us in many different ways, but always with the

---

[3] Shabbos 30b.

[4] Amalek refers to a nomadic people, the first to attack the Jewish people on their way to receive Torah (Shemos 17:6). The gematria of Amalek is suffek, which means "doubt," its sole purpose being to create doubt in belief in God and Divine Providence. Therefore Amalek is considered to be the nemesis, not just of the Jewish people, but of God Himself (Shemos 17:16).

[5] Shemos 17:8.

same purpose—to stop Jews from living a meaningful and mindful Torah life.

Hence Amalek was the first nation to attack the Jewish people, right before they arrived at Mt. Sinai to receive the Torah. Why? Because its existence depends on a weak connection between Jews and Torah. Thus its first attack was at Refidim, which means "weak in the hands." Amalek was able to attack the Jewish people because Torah was weak in the hands of our nation.[6]

Therefore, if the Torah were given to the Jewish people to promote mindFULness, then it is Amalek's sole purpose to promote just the opposite, mindLESSness. It could be something as simple—but terribly wasteful—as people losing their focus at precisely the time they need to have intention for a mitzvah, or something as far more profoundly damaging as subscribing to a mistaken idea. Either way, people will miss out on moments of reality.

Because that is what it is all about, being IN the moment—with ALL OF YOU. Life is a VERY long string of moments, each with its own potential to impart additional life to its user. The minutes move so fast that we barely even notice them, unless something happens to make us take note. Before we know it, a lifetime has passed and we can hardly remember most of

---

6 Bechoros 5b.

it.

What we do remember most easily and quickly are the events that demanded the most from us. Whether a traumatic experience or one that we wished would never end, we invested in it. We were intellectually AND emotionally there, and that seemed to engrave the experience deeper into our memory.

This is why so many people are prepared to take tremendous risks just to have fun, or spend so much money to do something like parachuting. The more exciting something is, the more of us it pulls into the moment. The more mindful we are, the more ALIVE we feel.

Movie producers know this and take full advantage of it to get people to pay good money to watch their films. This is what makes "good" entertainment so, well, entertaining. It has the ability to draw our intellect and emotions in, leaving us with a sense of the life we want to experience, even for only two hours at a time.

When it comes to Torah, few people think about it as being entertaining. On the contrary, Torah for many is very unentertaining. Some even have a difficult time paying just a small fee to access it, feeling that it should be free since they are making the supreme sacrifice of looking at it.

Others, albeit a small minority, know differently. They know that Torah is the MOST entertaining of all, not in the secular sense of the term, but in its ULTI-MATE sense. They are not only drawn to Torah but have a very difficult time parting from it.

Hence the Torah says:

> I have set before you life and death, the blessing and the curse. Choose life, so that you and your offspring will live… (Devarim 30:19)

Choose life? Would healthy people choose anything else? Yes, if they did not fully understand what living means. Yes, if they thought that it is better to give in to the body and sleep than listen to the soul and get up on time for minyan. Yes, if they thought that it is more enjoyable to be spaced out while praying rather than working hard to concentrate and FEEL the prayers.

Funny how when it comes to making money or becoming famous, people accept working hard. They make great sacrifices and focus intensely on what they are doing. Their success requires it, and if they want one, they know that they have to accept the other, as well as the many rituals that come with it.

But not when it comes to religion, and especially the 613 *mitzvos* of Torah. They don't buy what the rabbis have written:

> The Tablets are the handiwork of God, and the

script was God's script charus–engraved on the Tablets. Do not read charus, but rather cheirus– freedom. For no person is more free than one who engages in Torah study. (Pirkei Avos 6:2)

People who don't accept this do not understand TRUE freedom. There is freedom and then there is freedom. There is the freedom to do whatever you feel like doing, which is usually a *yetzer-hara* thing. Then there is the freedom to be the very best you can be, a *yetzer-tov* thing, which is what the Torah speaks to.

In short, Torah focuses people on the greatest part of being human, and provides the most effective path to achieve it. It demands that people be mindful of their time and opportunities in life. It defines what is good and what is bad, so that people will know what is worthy of their attention and what should be ignored. In short, Torah encourages and inspires people to live up to their full potential. Can there be anything more liberating than this?

*   *   *

I had bought the book on Mindfulness at the airport in Atlanta while on my way to New York. There I had dinner with my brother-in-law, a retired executive from a premier insurance company and super-bright

Torah Jew. Since I enjoy sharing my ideas with him, I told him about the book and my Torah take on the topic.

His eyes lit up. Long before I bought the book, he had worked on similar material and put together his own presentation for employees at his company. We concurred on a number of points, and I picked up some direction from what he had already thought through. It was quite extensive.

Two days later, about to leave for the airport to return to Israel, my brother-in-law spoke to me about an exciting idea. It occurred to him that perhaps we could collaborate on a book. He was only interested in getting his ideas out there where they could help people. Not wanting to write the book himself, he asked me to use his material, edit it as I saw fit, and finally publish it.

I shared his excitement because the idea had occurred to me as well, though I didn't yet have enough nerve to suggest it. My plan was to write something, send it to him for feedback, and then draw him into the project if I could. I was pleasantly surprised to hear that he was, on his own, on board.

What follows is that collaboration. The first seven chapters of this book are based largely on his material. I just created the storyline as a way of presenting the ideas in a mindful and attention-keeping manner.

We hope that it will help the reader relate to the material even more personally.

MAJESTIC, ISN'T IT, how water rises from the surface of the sea and in a short time becomes a sparkling, glass-like wave. It begins small, but can grow quite large and become breathtaking in its own right. And though it remains dependent on the sea beneath for existence, it can give the impression of being quite independent.

But only for a short while. The gradual whiteness forming at its peak is a sign that the wave is slowing down, losing momentum. Soon it will fall back to the surface of the sea from which it came and become a thunderous "breaking" wave. Full of sound and fury, it will crash and charge the shore, creating whiteness and foam all around.

Each breaking wave seems to be an autonomous entity, striving for glory and power. For a time it seems to exist somewhat apart from its source, drawing attention only to itself, smashing anything in its path. Yet in a few minutes its momentum and strength will diminish, slightly at first but then rapidly. Its coherence gone, it is quieted, and its whiteness decomposes into thousands of tiny bubbles, each going its own way, struggling in vain to survive.

Finally the breaking wave meekly turns back, as it is pulled from the shore once again into the sea. Sheepishly it returns to its source, underneath the next approaching breaking wave that is now stealing the stage and which will also soon suffer the same fate.

It is easy to think that all that matters are the roaring waves, one after the other, with their noise and tumult, despite their pathetically short life span. After all, they ceremoniously proclaim their presence and dramatically grab our attention. But it is not true that the waves are all that matter, because they are only temporary, while the sea—which gives rise to the waves—is still there. The sea may be quiet, but it always endures and is the source of each loud wave.

To really see the sea we need to look beyond the crashing waves. But how does one avoid being captivated by the breaking waves, and connect instead to the sea that is profoundly greater?

There is a way. Sometimes a wave can rise and move toward the shore without leaving its basic state. It can roll in until the very last minute and then gently touch the shoreline, with no noise, no pounding, no destruction, no whiteness, no decomposition into dissipating bubbles. Waves like this may seem to lack the power of breaking waves, but they have something else that the largest, noisiest, attention-grabbing waves can never have: a continuous bond with the sea.

An Analogy for Life

The sea-wave scenario has something to say about life as well. It is a good analogy to help us better understand our time in this world and the people living in it. In fact the sea can be said to be analogous to the universal consciousness of God from which all souls come and to which all souls remain connected, even after they enter bodies and live in this world.

Each individual soul, a portion of divine light, is like a majestically rising wave. It is part of the sea and at the same time a thing of beauty and majesty in its own right. Yet once in this world, it does not seem able to sustain its existence solely in its pure, pristine state. This is evident by how many souls seem to make so much noise and cause so much damage while here.

We are clearly capable of other states of mind that seem to have a nature entirely different from our pure soul. And the babble of thoughts they generate are so often like breaking waves: self-centered and all consuming, oblivious of the transcendence and the miracle that gave birth to them. They can walk over anything in their path, and seem opposed to any sense of connection to something larger than themselves.

But just like a breaking wave, the stream of individual, destructive, incoherent thoughts that for one moment seem so tenacious and relentless will eventually dissolve and disintegrate into nothingness. And so will the second wave of such thinking, and the third, and so on.

Unfortunately though, for many people the repetitive and endless stream of random, self-centered thoughts end up defining how they experience life. Their way of thinking suppresses any connection to something larger than the individual thoughts themselves, as temporal and insubstantial as they are.

A Different Way of Thinking

It is important to know, however, that there is a type of thinking that is not ego-driven and desirous of glory, that can change all this. It is a thinking that is connected, empathetic, creative, receptive, caring. It is a way of thinking that doesn't sever its ties to the essential mind nor to the soul from which it came.

This kind of thinking is quiet and does not draw

attention to itself. It doesn't make the same immediate impression as louder, more self-centered thinking seems to do. But it is the source of our greatest insights, our most richly lived moments, and our greatest connection to others.

Because this way of thinking doesn't lose its connection to the soul, it reflects who we TRULY are. It is the experience of such thinking that allows us to see more clearly the constant truth—that we are much more than our noisy thoughts. We are conscious souls connected to God, Who gave us the wondrous ability to think.

If we maintain a constant connection to this truth, then our thoughts as well will come to take on a different character. They will become more coherent, richer, caring, and less ego-focused. Like the wave that remains pristine throughout its journey to the shore, our thoughts will themselves better reflect the inherent nature of their source: our pure and godly soul.

HE HAD NOTICED the change weeks before but assumed it was temporary. With most boys he would have felt comfortable just asking straight out what was troubling them, but not Yirmi. He was the sensitive type, lacking the same thick skin as the rest of his friends. There had to be MORE than due cause to pry into his personal life.

Was he not feeling well? Was something going on at home? He wasn't sure. One thing he WAS sure of was how easy it is to misread people, something he had come to learn the hard way from all the times he found out how well he did NOT know one boy or another, after assuming he had.

People have their secrets, all of us. We have an inner face and an outer one, and that's usually a good thing. Why should one person's dour mood bring down other people? A face is in the public domain, one rabbi taught. You have to be constantly aware of how it affects others, and personal privacy usually demands that we are.

But sometimes the inner world of people is in turmoil, more chaotic than they can handle on their own. It becomes all-consuming, until they can no longer keep it to themselves. That's when it starts to spill over into the outside world, and the outer face begins to take on the appearance of the inner face. Clearly that had happened to Yirmi.

How many times had students made appointments with him and poured out their hearts about issues that he, their mentor and guide, had no idea about? Not only on one occasion did he sit in his chair, listening intently to the young man across from him, TOTALLY caught off guard by what he was hearing. It made him wonder how many others had similar stories behind THEIR smiles.

At 2 p.m. he hoped to learn Yirmi's story. He had asked him to come to his office at that time just to check in, something he had the boys do on a regular basis. He wanted to be accessible to all of them on an ongoing basis, to avoid situations like the one Yirmi was going through. He wanted to practice preventive medicine, and not have to respond to crises that had already occurred.

In the meantime yeshivah issues consumed his time, which he completely lost track of. When the knock came at 2 p.m. exactly, he thought it was his secretary, and unconsciously called out, "Yes?"

The door opened slightly, and he still hadn't looked up from his work, expecting to hear the secretary's voice. Instead he heard, "Rabbi Lowenstein, you wanted to see me?"

Caught off guard, he looked up, not immediately recognizing the voice since he was expecting a different one.

"Yirmi," he said, immediately transferring his attention from the matter on his desk to the matter at the door. "Come on in…thanks for coming…and on time yet. I really appreciate that."

"Sure," Yirmi answered, closing the door behind him and taking the seat the rabbi motioned to him.

The rabbi sat back in his reclining chair and reminded himself to be patient.

"I just wanted to see how you are doing," he said, "You know, your yearly check-up..

Yirmi smiled, recognizing the dental jargon.

"Good, Boruch Hashem," he answered halfheartedly, revealing nothing, as was expected.

"How's the learning?"

"Also good, Boruch Hashem," he continued, camouflaging all.

"And you're okay with the dorm?" the rabbi said, assessing the young man before him, and wondering how to get through his armor.

"Sure," Yirmi said, obviously insincerely. EVERY-ONE had complaints about the dorms. Most of the boys came from good homes that lacked for nothing. The dorm was an easy comedown. "I mean…it's not like home…but it's just a dorm. It's good enough."

The rabbi smiled. Even in his own pain, he was considerate of others, telling his rabbi what he wanted to hear, rather than what he wanted to tell him.

"Great," he said, almost sounding dismissive. Yirmi even thought that was all he was there for, but the awkward moment of silence that followed seemed to suggest otherwise, making him feel the need to squirm in his seat.

Finally, the rabbi leaned forward onto his desk, cutting the distance between them in half. He looked right into Yirmi's eyes, which made him immediately feel exposed. But he kept everything inside just the same, forcing the rabbi to find his own way in.

The eye contact became so intense that Yirmi had to look away. He knew what was coming next, and considered lying. But he was one of the most honest kids around, and clearly his lie would not pass detection. He began to feel trapped.

Rabbi Lowenstein was known to be empathetic,

and he could sense the inner turmoil the young student was experiencing. So sat back in his chair again, trying to appear super relaxed in order to let up somewhat and give the boy some breathing room. He even smiled to imply, "Everything is good."

"Yirmi," he finally said. "I wouldn't have thought much of it if it weren't you."

Yirmi looked up quizzically.

"You're one of our best students with one of the biggest hearts I've ever seen, even in adults."

The compliment threw him off and was strangely soothing.

"I mean, I've seen you doven."

Yirmi was clearly embarrassed.

"Obviously you know Whom you are talking to, and take it seriously…It's inspiring to other boys!"

Yirmi wondered how true that was, but the rabbi helped him out.

"I've had other boys sit in that chair and tell me how much they wished they could doven the same way as you."

Now Yirmi blushed.

"I didn't mean to embarrass you," the rabbi said, "but I mention it because I have noticed lately that you don't seem as…inspired…when it comes to dovening. Rabbi Dworski even tells me that you have come late on a few occasions…and that's not like you!"

Yirmi eyes did not leave the floor. He said nothing, at a loss for words. The problem was that he was worried about being kicked out of yeshivah…or just sent home. He knew the yeshivah had enough problems without having to worry about some mentally imbalanced student, which is how he thought of himself.

On the other hand, the problem was getting worse. He had had it for years, but was always able to deal with it somewhat. He didn't know why, but it seemed to become more intense with each passing year. It had gone from just bugging him occasionally to interfering with his general happiness, even disrupting his prayers and learning. And he didn't know what to do about it.

"Yirmi, my son," the rabbi said. "Is everything REALLY okay?"

There was something about the rabbi's voice, its inherent sympathy and care, that broke down his defenses. To his amazement, he began to cry…and cry… and cry. Completely humiliated, he put his face on his arm, and tried with all his might to stop this childish behavior. Now for sure he was out.

Finally, after a few minutes, he slowly looked up at the rabbi, wondering what he had been doing the entire time he himself was reverting to early childhood. Had he gone back to thinking about his work, which would explain his lack of response?

What he saw confused him enough to distract

him from his own feelings, and he stopped crying. There were tears running down the rabbi's face. He made no effort to hide them or make excuses for himself. And all of a sudden Yirmi no longer felt so alone, so cut off in his past. His own tears even felt justified.

Yirmi's face indicated that he wondered why the rabbi had responded like that, but out of respect, he would not ask. So the rabbi volunteered the information himself.

"Yirmi, your pain is MY pain."

Yirmi felt his whole body relax with those words, even though he had no time to process them. It was as if his muscles had feelings of their own.

"And I am so HONORED and RELIEVED that you feel comfortable enough with me…trust me enough… to actually share such personal feelings."

Those words were extremely comforting. And Yirmi felt not just comforted, but hopeful. Until then he had shared his problem with NO ONE, which gave him the disparaging feeling that there was no solution. For the first time in months, maybe even years, he had a sense of hope…of redemption. He shared that with the rabbi through his facial expression.

The rabbi took a deep breath and continued. "Okay. Now that we have gotten all that out of the way, let's talk."

Yirmi also took a deep breath and sat back as he considered where to start and how much to divulge.

After all, how did he know that the rabbi still wouldn't throw him out of yeshivah once he heard his actual story? He didn't. But he had gone too far now, and NOT opening up at that point would look even worse, so he might as well focus instead on what to say.

He took another deep breath and exhaled, "It's my thoughts."

"They're bothering you," the rabbi said matter of factly.

Yirmi hadn't known what to expect in return, but it certainly wasn't such a casual response. It wasn't even a question but a statement, as if this were no big deal to him. There was something reassuring just in that.

"A LOT," he said.

The rabbi put two and two together and continued.

"And they bother you especially when you *doven*."

"Yes," he found himself saying without even thinking.

"So much so that you're afraid to *doven* at all…"

"Exactly!" All of a sudden, the mysterious was seeming less mysterious.

"Which makes you feel even worse, because you love to doven."

Now Yirmi looked up at his rebi. He was getting too much right too fast. Was he actually a mind reader?

"No, I'm not a mind reader," the rabbi said, sensing his wonderment, which made Yirmi even more convinced that he was.

"What, you think you're the only one?" the rabbi asked, purposely downplaying the problem. "Been there, done that," he said, smiling.

"You've had the same problem?"

"Not only me, but a whole lot of other boys who have sat in that chair over the years."

"Really?" Yirmi said, incredulous. Until now he had suffered alone. He had assumed that no normal person had his problem.

"What did they do to deal with it?" he asked. "What did the rav do to deal with it?"

"Well, for a while I just ignored it. But then it began to interrupt my dovening, and it would rear its ugly head while I was learning. I would be learning beautifully, and then all of a sudden random and weird thoughts would just pop into my head. Sometimes something in the *Gemora* or *tefillah* would trigger some memory, which would trigger some thought, and then another, and…"

"EXACTLY!" Yirmi said, almost as if in a trance, reliving his own recent episode. "It's taken all the joy out of my learning…and put so much fear into my life! I mean, where do these thoughts come from? I certainly don't want them…but I don't know how to stop them. The harder I try, the worse they seem to get!"

"I have good news for you," the rabbi said, folding his hands as he sat back in his chair. "The problem is real."

Yirmi took a deep breath.

"But so is the solution."

He exhaled slowly, far more relaxed.

"What do I have to do?" he asked, eager to get started. "I can't WAIT to get back to dovening with the proper kavanah[7] again…and to learn undistractedly."

The rabbi was one step ahead of him. He had opened his desk drawer and was shuffling through some papers, smiling as he found what he was looking for. He put the tattered paperback on the desk in front of him, and Yirmi's eyes went right to it. Then he slowly moved it toward him, at which time Yirmi looked back at the rabbi.

"It looks used," Yirmi said, knowing why.

"Very," the rabbi said. "In fact, rarely a week goes by that I don't look at this book myself…that is, when I haven't lent it out."

Yirmi's eyes shifted back and forth between the book and the rabbi.

"May I?" he asked politely.

"By all means."

Yirmi reached for the book and studied the cover.

---

[7] Intention.

"Mindfulness," he said softly. "*Mind* the Moment, *Mine* the Opportunity."

Yirmi flipped through the worn pages and was intrigued by all the underlining and annotations on almost every page.

"Those are my own notes," the rabbi explained. "They're for me, but feel free to read them if you like."

Yirmi looked at the rabbi for a moment, to acknowledge his words.

"You can borrow it," he told Yirmi. "For three days."

Yirmi looked at the rabbi, surprised by the very short amount of time he could use the book.

"Because that's all it will take before you decide to buy your own indispensable copy."

Yirmi smiled while turning pages. In the meantime the rabbi sat back and gave him some time to leaf through the book, which was only 120 pages long. But he himself was thinking at the same time, and he came up with a new idea.

"And in two months I want you to teach it."

Yirmi's head jerked back. "What?"

"In two month I want you to give a class on this material to the rest of the boys. I'll arrange it with the mashgiach."[8]

"Wait, I can't teach…"

---

8 The person who oversees the *bais midrash*.

The rabbi cut him off mid-sentence.

"I think you can. In fact, I think you will be great at it, and you will help a lot of boys…who might not be as open as you have been today, but who suffer silently."

Yirmi thought about that for a moment, and an internal tug of war began. He loved to help people but he hated publicity. It wasn't his way. But the rabbi was telling him that it was a good thing to do.

"It would be REAL *chesed.*" the rabbi added for added impact and persuasion.

Yirmi thought for a moment and was grateful for the compromise that came to his mind out of nowhere.

"Can I look at the book for a few days first and see if the material helps me? Then I will let the rav know if I think I can work with this…perhaps even give it over to a couple of boys at a time."

"Sounds like a plan," the rabbi agreed.

It would be great if something actually came of it. But the rabbi's immediate intention was for the sake of the boy, to distract him with the project and give him something else to think about, something positive, instead of his random, disturbing thoughts. It was part of the therapy.

"Great," Yirmi said, preparing to end the session. "Thank you so much for your time. You have been a great help for me."

"That's what I'm here for," the rabbi told him.

Yirmi got up to make his way to the door, so the rabbi added, "And Yirmi…"

"Yes?"

"Please don't ever hesitate to share with me, or any of the other rabbis here, what's on your mind, WHATEVER it is."

He looked down at his shoes, again embarrassed.

"You're one of our brightest and most talented students, capable of doing a lot for the Jewish people. You have a VERY large heart, what every great leader needs. We're here to work with you…to help you develop. You can count on that…ALWAYS. You, and all the other students that learn at this yeshivah. Okay?"

"Okay," Yirmi confirmed, placing the book in his inside jacket pocket.

"I look forward to hearing from you in three days."

Yirmi smiled and bowed his head in acknowledgment, then turned and left, softly closing the door behind him.

Looking at the back of the door, Rabbi Lowenstein reviewed the entire session in his head. His first reaction was concern, but then he smiled to himself and thought, "He's going to be just fine," and returned to the more mundane matters in front of him on the desk. As he did, some random thoughts flooded his head, but he just said, "No thank you," and went back to work. Soon his young protégé would be able to do the same.

"COGITO ERGO SUM is a Latin philosophical pro-position by René Descartes,[9] usually translated into English as 'I think, therefore I am.' As Descartes explained, 'we cannot doubt of our existence while we doubt.'"

"That's not MY problem," Yirmi said. "Mine is more like…I think, therefore…I am aggravated."

"It isn't uncommon for people to question their existence. The brain has a difficult time distinguishing between dream state and reality, and if a person be-

---

[9] René Descartes (1596-1650) was a French philosopher, mathematician, and scientist.

comes overly mindful of the two states, they can take on a dreamlike quality. This can confuse the brain and the person."

"Not my problem," Yirmi insisted.

"This is not the case for most people though. Many are not mindful ENOUGH of their reality, and kind of live on autopilot. They figure that as long as they are breathing and getting around, they are living fully. The sad truth is that most of life just passes them by."

This time Yirmi wondered if that might apply to him somewhat. Then he realized that that's one of the benefits of living by Torah. Torah MAKES you mindful…or at least TRIES to. Although it's still quite possible to do mitzvos on autopilot as well.

"Then again, for others, it's the thoughts themselves that are the problem."

His eyes widened. "That's EXACTLY my problem!" he loudly blurted out, quickly looking around to see if anyone heard him.

"If this is you, then you are bothered by all kinds of random thoughts…thoughts that you do not recognize."

"EGGactly," he agreed. "NOW we're on the same page."

"You are disturbed because they come at the worst times."

"I'll say."

"And some are scary."

"VERY."

"They make you wonder who you really are, and how you can possibly have such thoughts."

Ouch. That was a tender spot. "Exactly," he repeated, this time without the comic tone and under his breath.

"This makes you feel even more isolated, cut off from the 'normal' world…as if you belong in some kind of mental facility…and wondering how long it will be until someone discovers your secret and turns you in."

"Yeah," he said, feeling fear coursing through every vein in his body.

There was a long moment of silence, and then the GOOD news.

"Well, as one American president said, 'The only thing we have to fear is…fear itself!'[10] You have to know that all that fear and all that suffering are really just the result of a lack of understanding and some truly misguided thinking. And the really good news? Once you clear up both, the problem will more or less take care of itself, as it has for so many already."

"GREAT," Yirmi said, "I'm all ears."

Then he corrected himself, "I mean I'm all EYES."

Even though his rosh yeshivah had given the

---

[10] Franklin D. Roosevelt's first inaugural address, March 4, 1933.

book to him and it was written from a Torah perspective, he didn't feel comfortable reading it in the bais midrash, not even during lunch break. Instead, he took it with him to his favorite sandwich shop close to the yeshivah, found a table out of the way, and read while he ate. It was more relaxing there, and he needed that to concentrate these days.

"It would help to know how our thoughts work," the author continued. "The mistaken assumption is that if WE think about something, then WE must be behind the thought. It must have originated from us."

"And that's not true?" Yirmi asked, as if talking to the author in person.

"That is true to some extent, but only when we CONSCIOUSLY choose to think about something."

Yirmi liked that. He took another bite and read more.

"Some people call them earworms, some call them mind-pops, but random thoughts that enter your brain for no apparent reason are actually important, according to scientists. Our brains can surprise us with sudden random memories. It could be a line from a play from 6th grade that you were in or a song from a commercial that you saw last week."

"Not me," Yirmi said to himself. "I wasn't in any play in 6th grade, and I didn't hear a song from a commercial last week."

"The complete unpredictability of these thoughts

is a fun part of being human."

"Fun? Are you kidding? Maybe for you, but certainly not for me."

"Even when scientists have explored almost all our grey matter, they are still able to learn new things that we are capable of. We are constantly amazed by our brains."

"Perhaps," Yirmi interrupted, "but personally, I have many things to be fascinated by, and random thoughts are NOT on that list. Where do they come from?"

The author continued.

"Stray or random thoughts are what scientists call involuntary semantic memories. These thoughts are involuntary, meaning they are not something you were trying to think of. Semantic refers to facts or events, but the word itself means 'meaning.' These random thoughts are memories that come back to you when you aren't expecting them, and they have no apparent meaning. The most interesting part of these random thoughts is that they might not be random after all. Scientists think that these memories are trying to help you solve a problem."

"SOLVE a problem?" Yirmi thought to himself. "MINE only CREATE problems."

"Problem solving is one way that scientists believe our random mind-pops are benefitting us. In fact, a seemingly random thought can often be traced back to a particular trigger. Scientists believe that random thoughts are likely the result of memory processing and also creative thinking. You may start to notice that you have mind-pops more often when you have a problem that you want to solve."

"Actually, just the opposite," Yirmi disagreed. "My random thoughts tend to attack me when I'm trying to focus on something important…like during *Shema* or *Shemoneh Esrai*…There's no PROBLEM that I'm trying to solve then…other than trying to be real with the words."

The author seemingly ignored the comment and continued in spite of it.

"It's as if you have told your brain, albeit unwittingly, to search for things that can help you solve the problem, and your brain responds with random thoughts that are, as far as the brain is concerned, connected. Researchers speculate that mind-pops are the results of long-term semantic priming,[11] with an initial exposure to a source of information activating a web of representations in the mind that stay activated until a relevant stimulus in our environment triggers the semantic memory."

---

[11] Semantic priming refers to the observation that a response to a target (e.g., dog) is faster when it is preceded by a semantically related prime (e.g., cat), as compared to an unrelated prime (e.g., car).

He took some time to digest that thought, and read the paragraph several times. "Hmm," he said. "That IS true. Something usually does trigger the thoughts…though I don't understand how or why. Sometimes the harder I try to concentrate, the more the unwanted thoughts come."

The book continued.

"The tenuous relationship between some of these initial activation experiences and the semantic memories that result from them minutes, hours, and even days later"—or YEARS later, Yirmi thought— "hints at a correlation between mind-popping and creative thinking, an ability to perceive connections between seemingly unrelated concepts."

"That's interesting," Yirmi thought. "I never looked at it as creative thinking…mostly because I didn't like what was being created."

He ate the last bite of his sandwich, took a final drink, and sat back to contemplate.

"Just imagine," he thought, and as he did, he became awed. "I really only CONSCIOUSLY think about the present, or the immediate past or future. But my brain…it's a VAST storehouse and network of countless ideas and experiences…maybe millions… that I couldn't access even if I tried."

He did the math. He was 17 years old, which means he had already lived for more than 6,000 days.

"That is a LOT, and all the experiences of those

days are recorded somewhere in the deepest recesses of my brain…connected in ways I can't begin to fathom…dormant until something triggers them and calls them up to my conscious mind!"

"I may have moved on and forgotten things," he continued to himself, "but my brain never did. My unconscious mind is the sum total of my life experience until today! That's awesome!"

"There's not another ME in there," he realized, "but rather a whole LIBRARY of thoughts and feelings that line shelf after shelf in my brain…just waiting to be actualized when called on by some…some…association, I guess. Wow," he felt, achieving new realizations. "My brain is a lot more creative than I am!"

He chuckled at the thought. Then something told him to look at his watch, and a good thing too. It was much later than he suspected, and Minchah was in 20 minutes. He still had to bentch[12] and get back to the yeshivah within 15 minutes, so he started to close the book. However, one more paragraph caught his attention.

"People who experience frequent random thoughts tend to rate higher on tests of creative thinking. In a study of the brains of research subjects and their random thoughts, high-frequency mind-pops were significantly associated with a larger volume of

---

[12] Say blessings after a meal.

grey-and-white matter in the prefrontal cortex. This increase in mind-pops is also linked to higher creativity and the personality trait of openness."

"Well, that is fascinating," he said, reaching for his jacket and hat to bentch. He wasn't sure he understood all of it, but there was something complimentary in it anyhow. And reassuring, because he began to feel a separation taking place between him and his unconscious thoughts. "I am NOT my thoughts," he intoned to himself, "and my thoughts are NOT me."

It was as if his unconscious thoughts came from the head of someone else. They were the result of myriad experiences and exposures, most of which he had no control over, and which he may or may not have understood at the time. Yet his brain was built to file them ALL, to store them for possible future use if ever needed.

And the brain tags everything to the best of its ability, right or wrong. That's what allows future access on demand…sometimes incorrectly…or at the most inappropriate times. The brain is just doing what it was built to do, leaving it up to the conscious mind to decide what to use and what to reject.

When the brain gets it right, we don't notice it, because it doesn't bother us. When our unconscious thoughts come up at the RIGHT time, we don't pay much attention. When they lead to a solution, we just assume everything is normal. We don't consider that these "good" thoughts are part of the same program that produces the "bad" thoughts. It's a package deal.

Yirmi *bentched*, trying to have as much *kavanah*[13] as he could. He was overwhelmed by all the recent insights, and his body tingled with the excitement of finally finding a path out of his personal nightmare. He got up, put the book back into the inner pocket of his jacket, and headed for the door. On the way out he made a point to thank his friend behind the counter, feeling more like himself than he had in a long time.

He thought about reading some more while he walked, but knew it would only slow him down. Instead, he considered how his new understanding would impact *Minchah*. Or, he wondered, would it take time before the ideas settled in enough to beat back years of mistaken thinking?

He looked at his watch.

In three minutes he would have his answer.

---

[13] Concentration and intention.

MINCHAH WENT SURPRISINGLY well. The random and unwanted thoughts continued to come, but Yirmi didn't panic. He didn't even fight them. Instead he simply waited patiently for the thoughts to dissipate After a while they stopped coming and he resumed his tefillah.

When thoughts returned, he did the same thing. He told himself, "These thoughts are not me…They're just my brain doing its thing, unaware of whether it's appropriate or inappropriate. It just wants to help." By the time he completed these sentences, the thoughts had already stopped and he finished his dovening.

Learning *seder* also went well. He no longer felt

the need to get up and run away. The fear was gone, just like that. He was eager to get back to the book to learn more, but he also felt a newfound patience to wait until the appropriate time. Something inside told him that everything was going to be okay. It would take time, but he would be just fine. That was welcome news.

One dinnertime his usual place at the table was empty. His best friend and chavrusa briefly wondered where he was. Although it wasn't uncommon for someone to skip yeshivah food and go for an upgrade, Yirmi usually asked him to go with him.

Yirmi knew his presence would be missed but wasn't concerned. He picked up something from the local store to snack on while delving more into the book in a quiet corner in the middle of nowhere. He wanted to know more. He NEEDED to know more.

He took plenty of notes. They were mostly for him, but would also be useful if he took his rosh yeshivah up on the offer to teach the material to others. The idea made him uncomfortable, not the teaching part, which he enjoyed, but rather the topic and the need to open up to others who would do the same.

On the other hand, he realized that sharing the material with others would make it more real to him, perhaps drive it deeper into his consciousness. He wasn't looking for a bandaid solution. He wanted a permanent one, and teaching the ideas would force him to learn them thoroughly, and think about them a lot. That appealed to him.

In any case, there was still time to deal with that problem. The more immediate issue was getting a better handle on the material and implementing it. He had already noticed significant improvement, and he wanted to see more. Comfortable, with snack in hand, he picked up where he last left off.

"The trick is to maximize random thoughts to your benefit," the book said. "Being mindful is the best way to use random thoughts to enhance your creativity. Here are a few ideas to help you allow your random thoughts to solve problems for you."

He liked that idea. He was creative by nature, something he had always considered to be an asset. It allowed him to find solutions others could not, and to gain insights that others often overlooked. He had written articles that were praised by others for their creativity, and that encouraged him to be even more creative.

Now he was learning that this tendency was a double-edged sword. The creative ability is always working in the background, doing things that he did not necessary want or need to think about. He had instinctively fought against that, which only intensified the problem. Now he was learning that the better way was to figure out how to harness those thoughts for some greater good.

"Dwell on the random thought for 90 seconds, and immerse yourself in the memories that are brought up. Like them or hate them, our memories are part of us…part of what has shaped us into the person we are today. Trying to suppress memories that haunt us just makes them stick around longer, or come back even stronger at a later time. Staying with a memory and assessing its usefulness not only allows the memory to move on, but it also allows you to be who you are today."

He gave that some thought. He understood the idea, though he didn't know how practical it would always be, for him at least. Was he supposed to stop in the middle of *Shemoneh Esrai* and think about something totally unrelated or totally inappropriate? In the middle of a discussion with his *chavrusa*, was he going to allow himself to drift away each time some mind-pop appeared? Not likely.

But almost as if in response to his thinking, the answer suddenly came to him. He would carry a little notepad in his pocket. If some memory or idea came up that he needed to consider, but not at that time, he would jot it down and look at it later. He could afford a short interruption to avoid having a longer one.

"Living in the present is really what mindfulness is all about. This means not dwelling on the past and not worrying about the future, which people naturally do very well. Life is not in the past and it certainly isn't in the future. The present is the result of the past and has the ability to affect the future. But there is no sense trying to spend an inappropriate amount of the present on a past that cannot be changed or on the future which cannot be known."

That was so true. In the last two days he noticed more than ever how many things from the past popped up, and how much he worried about the future.

"So *bitachon*,"[14] he told himself, "not only means to trust in God for your future—it's also about investing your life in the present. You can't really live in the present if you're constantly thinking about the future or if you're dwelling in the past. Life is not really where your body presently is—it's where your mind is."

He wrote that down.

It occurred to him that this was a major advantage that Torah and *mitzvos* offer to those who keep them, and keep them properly. They focus you on the moment, just as a crisis does. They MAKE you live in the moment. There are specific acts designed to be carried out in very specific ways and at very specific times. You can't afford to be distracted if you want to get them right.

Take Shabbos for example. One day a week we

---

14 Trust in God.

have to stop all our weekday work and focus only on Shabbos. We have to prepare in advance for it so we can enjoy it, and we have to honor it by the way we dress and act. It's like closing the file on the previous week and transitioning to the next one.

We have Rosh Chodesh. Every month we have to do something different, just for Rosh Chodesh. How can you NOT notice the passage of time with that? Or with a New Year designed to make you take a good, hard look at the previous year in preparation for the next one?

Then of course there is dovening. *Shacharis* by a certain time. *Minchah* by a certain time. *Ma'ariv* by its own certain time. Most people today probably don't care all that much about sunrise or sunset, but a Torah Jew has to. His life pretty much has to be in sync with the different times of the day. How much more mindfulness practice can you get?

"Hmm," he thought. "That's what they really mean when they say that freedom is engraved on the tablets.[15] *Mitzvos* ARE freedom!"

He let himself absorb those words. He loved learning and for the most part had no problem performing the *mitzvos*. But this added a whole new dimension to both, and he wanted to share that idea with others who struggled with them every day.

---

[15] Pirkei Avos 6:62.

"After all, what is freedom?" he asked rhetorically. "The freedom to do whatever you feel like doing when you feel like doing it? It certainly seems like that to billions of people! But if you asked them what they wanted the most from life, they would probably answer something like 'to live it to the fullest.' That's what I want. I want to know that when I leave this world, I was the very best ME I could be…and I can only do that if I'm getting out of each moment of my life the most of me. That's what mitzvos do…if you think about them and do them right."

"I agree," his *chavrusa* said, almost causing him to fall off the bench. First of all, he hadn't realized that he had been speaking so loudly and, secondly, in his isolated location he hadn't expected to be heard by anyone.

"How did you find me?' he asked his good friend of many years. "How did you know I was here?"

"I didn't," his friend told him. "I was actually on my way back to the dorm to get a *sefer*. I didn't see you anywhere, so I thought I would run back and get it. I don't usually go this way, but there was a kind of traffic jam of people the regular way, so…"

"Anyhow," Yirmi said casually, to make it seem as if he were not so taken aback, "I was just about ready to pack up and go to the bais."

His friend Dovid looked at the book in his hand and the wrappers from what he had eaten.

"That was your supper?" he asked.

"A snack," he said. "I had a big lunch so I just wanted a snack for now. I'll get something else later."

"What's with the book?" he asked Yirmi, motioning with his head.

"It's just a book," he said.

"That much I can see. What kind of a book?"

Yirmi knew that being evasive would result in more mystery and questions, so he had to say something descriptive.

"A psychology book."

"A psychology book? Since when do you read psychology books?"

"Since the rosh yeshivah gave it to me."

"The rosh YESHIVAH gave you this psychology book? What is the rosh yeshivah even doing with a book on psychology…and why did he give it to you?"

"I don't have to tell him everything," Yirmi thought to himself.

"He wants me to prepare some classes on the material."

As the words left his mouth, he realized how strange it sounded and how it was going to lead to even more questions. So to head his friend off at the start, he ended with "How about continuing this conversation later? We're going to be late for seder if keep going now."

His friend looked at his watch and realized how

much time had passed. He had even lost the opportunity to get to the dorm and back, so they headed to the bais together, while Yirmi did his best to keep his friend distracted from the book and what he was doing with it. Maybe he'd forget the whole thing in a couple of hours.

He didn't. Just the opposite. He held himself back from speaking about it during their learning, but once the seder was over and they were returning to the dorm, he pressed Yirmi for details. Realizing that secrecy at that point would make things worse, not better, he decided to divulge some information, but not the distressing part.

"That's what the book is for?" Dovid asked, surprised. "I always have random thoughts. I usually start thinking about breakfast during Shemoneh Esrai."

Yirmi smiled. His friend tended to be humorous, and had a funny way of saying things.

"And that doesn't bother you?" Yirmi asked.

"Not as much as the other stuff that just HAPPENS to cross my mind at the most inopportune moments."

"Right."

"Yeah, but what's the big deal?" Dovid asked. "I just ignore it and go on."

"So do I," Yirmi said, a half-truth. "But I'd rather not have the thoughts at all."

"And that's what the book is for? To control your

thoughts?"

"Among other things." Yirmi answered.

"And THAT is what the rosh yeshivah wants you to teach…to the rest of us?"

"Among other things," he answered again.

"And that's supposed to help us in life?" he asked, and then quickly added, "And do NOT answer 'among other things' again, please."

Yirmi hadn't planned to, but couldn't help smiling nonetheless.

"What would you say if I told you there is so much from life that we could get if we just paid more attention?"

Dovid did that thing with his eyebrows that Yirmi came to realize indicated that he didn't understand what was just said and was now processing it.

"Okay," he finally said. "What is that supposed to mean? I mean I know that I don't get out of life all that I can…I'm not even thinking of getting married yet!"

"Yeah," Yirmi jumped in, "this will most DEFI-NITELY help with that…and with shalom bayis."

"Even though we haven't even fought yet?" Dovid kidded.

Without missing a beat, Yirmi answered, "You want to wait until then to work on it?"

"Hmm," Dovid said thoughtfully. "I guess you're right."

The two of them walked in silence for a few moments, each lost in his own thoughts.

"You need someone to test this stuff on?"

Yirmi thought for a moment. He had planned to go this alone as much as possible, but Dovid's idea had merit.

"Let me get started on this for now. As soon as I think I'm at a point to share it, you can be my first experimental laboratory subject," he said, rubbing his hands together with glee, while laughing diabolically.

"Save the theatrics for your audience," Dovid said nonchalantly.

"Sure," he said matter-of-factly as well, as they walked into their dorm.

An hour of hanging out and schmoozing before bedtime was normal for the six boys in the room, but one by one sleep overtook them. Except for Yirmi, that is, whose mind continued to race about the promise of a whole new and bold approach to life. It was exciting.

THREE DAYS PASSED quickly, and he was back in the rabbi's office, as planned. This time there was no small talk. The rosh yeshivah jumped right in, questioning Yirmi about his impressions so far, pressing him to turn the material into a course.

"This could be a future for you one day. It could be your parnassah!"[16] he told Yirmi excitedly, presenting the first carrot.

It was an interesting proposition, but not enticing enough. So the rosh yeshivah offered him a second carrot. From his top drawer he took a little black bind-

---

[16] Livelihood.

er, which had clearly been around for some time already, and placed it on the desk. He invited Yirmi to pick it up, which he did with respect.

Gently turning the worn pages, the handwriting was unmistakable. It was the rav's own personal notes, partly illegible. Some of them looked more like prescriptions for pharmaceutical products than life-altering ideas.

"These are the rav's own notes?" he asked, knowing the answer already.

"All of them," the rabbi answered, sitting back in his chair. "If you want to develop the course, they can help you. You can have full access to them whenever you want."

Yirmi looked up, clearly awed by the offer. It was getting harder to say no.

The rosh yeshivah then added the third carrot, "And we can meet for 45 minutes every week to discuss the material...until you feel you have it down pat."

Yirmi's resistance melted at that point. To have personal and ongoing access to such a great man would be the envy...well, at least the curiosity of the rest of the yeshivah...not that it was HIS reason to say yes.

"And," the rabbi kept pressing.

"And?" Yirmi thought to himself. "What ELSE could add to this once-in-a-lifetime opportunity?"

"You can call me any time you have a question."

"Any time?"

"Any time."

Yirmi was stunned. Clearly the rosh yeshivah was willing to invest much into his teaching of the material, and it made him wonder why.

"Please forgive me for asking, but it seems that the rav is willing to invest a lot of time and energy into the development of this course…May I ask why?"

The rabbi just grinned and said, "You may ask… but I will hold off with an answer…for now."

Yirmi was surprised by the response.

"Besides," he added, "I think the answer will become clear to you on your own…as we continue."

"Hmm," Yirmi thought to himself. "Mysterious."

Nevertheless he found himself saying, "I really can't say no, not with an opportunity to spend so much personal time with the rav. Besides, I'm the one who ultimately stands to benefit from all this."

With a knowing smile, the rosh yeshivah responded, "Great! This will be wonderful…for ALL of us."

"When do we start?" Yirmi asked, taking a deep breath.

The response was that "We already have."

*   *   *

The weeks flew by quickly. The more Yirmi learned, the more excited he became about the material. He particularly loved his time with the rosh yeshivah, and he decided to record their sessions so as to not slow them down with note-taking. He took notes later from the recording.

In the beginning they discussed the advantages of mindfulness that should be emphasized.

"For example, *tefillah*,"[17] the rav explained. "So many of the boys clearly struggle to doven.[18] They come late and finish early. It is such a pain for them, one which they will have to deal with for the rest of their lives."

"That's a LOT of boredom for a LOT of years," Yirmi said.

"Even worse. It's a lot of wasted time with the *Ribbono Shel Olam*."[19]

"Unfortunately," Yirmi conjectured, "I don't think a lot of people believe that they are really talking to God when they *doven*, or that He listens to what they are saying. They just don't take tefillah seriously. If they did, wouldn't they come on time and go more slowly? What could be better than talking to your Creator… especially since we depend on Him for every moment

---

[17] Prayer.

[18] Pray.

[19] Master of the Universe.

of our life?"

The rosh yeshivah liked what he was hearing.

"Exactly! They have no idea that they themselves are their worst problem. If they would only take the time to be more mindful of what they are doing, and what it means to them personally, they would come to LOVE *dovening!*"

"So how will this help them?"

"You already know the answer to that. I can see that by the way YOU doven."

Yirmi considered his own experience as his mentor continued.

"Something really mystical happens to *tefillah* when you just take the time to think about each of the words…We know that each word of *tefillah* was hand-picked by the *Anshei Knesses HaGedolah*,[20] many of whom were *nevi'im*.[21] They didn't just choose the words because that was the way people spoke. They chose each word because of its capacity to access higher realms, and combined them as they did…kabbalistically…to make them like spiritual…portals…to higher levels of spiritual consciousness."

There was a moment of silence while Yirmi absorbed the words, finally saying in awe, "Wow. I mean

---

[20] The 120 Men of the Great Assembly, who formalized and composed the prayers about 2,500 years ago.

[21] Prophets.

I've heard some of this before, but not expressed like that. How does it work?"

"The truth is that there are entire seforim written on the many kabbalistic intentions a person is supposed to have for each word of *tefillah*. Some are really complex and complicated, and it would take years to learn and understand them."

"But what are we supposed to do in the meantime?"

"That was part of the genius of Chazal[22] when they composed *tefillah*. They allowed access to the light of each *tefillah* to everyone according to the level he is on at the time."

"That's amazing."

"But the starting point," the rav said, "is wanting to enter the WORLD of *tefillah*, not just with your body, not just with your mind, but with your emotions as well. With your emotions ESPECIALLY."

"But how do you do that when you have all these outside thoughts bombarding you all the time? So much of the time it seems that the more I try to have kavanah, the more the thoughts interrupt me."

The rosh yeshivah leaned forward in his chair.

---

[22] A Hebrew acronym for the words "*Chachameinu zichronam livrochah*—our Wise Men, may they be remembered for brochah," which refers primarily to the rabbis of the Mishnaic and Talmudic Eras.

"When was the last time you went to a *chasa-nah*?"[23]

Yirmi thought for a moment. "Um…I think about two months ago."

"Did you enjoy it?"

Yirmi's face lit up as he instantly recalled the sim-chah and was transported back there.

"I mean, did you REALLY enjoy it?"

Still smiling, Yirmi said, "I really DID."

"What about your random thoughts? Didn't they interfere with your joy?"

Yirmi thought about that too and said, "Actually, I don't remember having any."

"EXACTLY," the rav said, sitting back in his chair again. "And do you know why?"

It didn't take much time for him to come back with an answer. "Because I was too busy having a good time to have any random thoughts."

"Right! In other words, you were 100 percent in the moment. The excitement of a *chasanah* will do that to you—it will pull ALL of you into the moment!"

Yirmi digested the thought, and the rav contin-ued.

"Now imagine if that were your *tefillah* experi-ence!"

"I wish I could. There is a big difference between

---

23 Hebrew for "wedding."

a loud and lively wedding and a quiet and stationary tefillah. A wedding is too distracting for silly random thoughts. Dovening…you're like a sitting…I mean a STANDING duck."

"Very true," the rabbi conceded. "But only in the beginning. The mind is a very powerful tool. It can be harnessed and used to accomplish powerful things."

"I LOVE the idea!" Yirmi said. "Does the rav have an example of how?"

"Yes. This is something I myself started doing a few years back."

Yirmi felt honored to be privy to such personal information.

"When I began the *Shemoneh Esrai*,[24] my brain would sometimes decide on its own to think about all the concerns and tasks I had planned to leave back in my office. And it seemed that the harder I tried to forget about them, the more they would insist on being heard."

"Yeah, that sounds like me."

"It was really frustrating, and I needed a solution. No, I needed a distraction…AWAY from the distractions."

"So what did the rav do?"

"One day I got the idea to imagine the reality of

---

[24] The *Amidah*, said standing and silently. It consists of 19 blessings and is considered a central element of each tefillah.

the words."

Yirmi's face showed that he didn't quite understand what that meant, but the rabbi knew that he would very quickly get it.

"First of all, I completely slowed down. That gave me time to formulate images in my head, so that when I said '*Elokei Avraham*—God of Avraham,' I could picture Avraham being thrown into the fire in Ur Kasdim to prove his belief in God. Then I would try to feel what he might have felt at that time, and that actually moved my heart."

Yirmi tried it for himself as he listened. Immediately it worked for him too.

"The same thing when I got to '*Elokei Yitzchak*—God of Yitzchak.' I thought about Yitzchak being tied up for the *Akeidah*, and what he and Avraham must have been thinking about the moment that they had to prove their faith in God. On '*Elokei Ya'akov*,' I imagined Ya'akov and all his struggles, especially fighting with the Angel of Eisav the entire night…and how he never lost faith in God. That little bit of mindfulness pulls me in and makes me forget everything else."

Yirmi was drawn in too. It's as if the words were hypnotic suggestions to cause him to imagine the same realities for himself, and it moved him as well. When the rabbi paused, he snapped out of his brief contemplation and again looked at the rosh yeshivah.

"That starts to draw my emotions in, and by trying to feel just a little of the love the Avos[25] had for God, I can feel some of my own. Then my *tefillah* and I move closer to each other, making it a more personalized experience. The words become my own, and that's the key to a meaningful *tefillah* experience.

"Basically, *tefillah* has to be a place you WANT to be. If it's not, then it just becomes a place you DON'T want to be, so you will minimize the experience as much as possible.

"The truth is that this goes for ALL *mitzvos*…You have to want to be doing them, or you'll minimize them as well."

"If you look around the *bais midrash*," Yirmi noted, "you can see that there are some *bochurim*[26] for whom that is easy, and for others…well…let's just say they struggle A LOT."

"Granted there are different natures," the rav conceded. "But imagine if in the middle of doing some *mitzvah* half-heartedly, a booming voice were to come down from *shamayim*[27] and say, 'I give you life, and this is the way you do My *mitzvos*? I give you health, and this is the way you say your *brochah*[28] after using the bathroom? You want to find the perfect *shid-*

---

[25] Forefathers.

[26] Unmarried students.

[27] Heaven.

[28] Blessing.

duch,[29] and you treat My *mitzvos* like THAT?' Now WHAT do you think THAT person is going to do at that moment?"

"Panic!" Yirmi said, only half-joking.

"And after that?"

Yirmi thought for a moment and put himself in the shoes of the imaginary person. "He's certainly going to take his *mitzvos* more seriously…A LOT more seriously!"

"But why?" the Rosh Yeshiva asked. "What did the voice change?

"It made him more aware…"

"…of what he should have ALREADY known on his own," the rabbi finished. "But he didn't, and instead learned the scary way that how he does a *mitzvah* either benefits or hampers him. It is this knowledge…this mindfulness…that infuses the *mitzvos* with meaning they didn't have before…for him, at least."

"But isn't that like doing a *mitzvah* for the sake of receiving a reward?" Yirmi asked.

"It's more like doing a *mitzvah* for the sake of survival. It's not the highest level, but it's a start."

"What IS the highest level?"

"Doing a mitzvah because you LOVE God. Then every one you do is an ACT OF LOVE, and that completely draws you into it."

---

[29] Marriage partner.

"But what if someone doesn't FEEL love for God?"

"Well," the rabbi said, "that's where the Rambam comes in. He tells people what they have to do to develop their love of God. Or, more accurately, to get in TOUCH with their love of God."

Yirmi's face said it all: he needed an explanation.

"The Rambam, when he explains the *mitzvah* of love and fear of God, gives us advice on how to go about feeling it. Basically, people need to take the time to be MINDFUL of the world they live in…its INCREDIBLE beauty…the AWESOME wisdom God used to make Creation."

"Something that people take for granted all the time," Yirmi admitted.

"Amazingly, yes. It is beyond comprehension how we can live with so many miracles on a moment-to-moment basis, and act as if NOTHING is that miraculous! The Gemora points this out: 'The person for whom a miracle is done doesn't recognize the miracle.'"[30]

"That's SO true," Yirmi agreed.

"But, the Rambam reveals to us, it can easily be remedied by taking the time to recognize and appreciate the miracles. Once you do, love of God…and this is the important part…AUTOMATICALLY results…

---

[30] Niddah 31a.

as if it were there the entire time…dammed up behind a wall of apathy and confusion and distraction. Remove that dam and…"

"…the love just floods in."

"Exactly," the Rav said. "It's as Dovid *HaMelech* said, 'I will thank You for the awesome, wondrous way I was fashioned; Your works are wondrous, and my soul knows it very well.' That is, his soul…his inner consciousness…ALREADY knew it, and now he was consciously articulating it."[31]

"Just from being MINDFUL of the world," Yirmi said, mostly to himself.

"And not only that," the rabbi continued, "but it works the same way when we deal with other people. There is a *mitzvah* to judge a person to the side of merit,[32] because we tend NOT to. We are quick to judge other people based on what we see, and not necessary favorably. We want people to give us a chance to explain ourself, and yet we're not so ready to give others the chance to do the same!"

"Guilty as charged," Yirmi confessed.

The rabbi smiled and continued.

"Imagine what kind of world it would be if people weren't so quick to judge others, friends OR strangers…if we just got into the habit of suspending our

---

[31] Tehillim 139:8.
[32] Shabbos 97a; 127b.

opinions about people or things, and gave our brain some time to come up with more thoughtful responses. Basically this happens quite naturally if we hold back on judgment. Believe it or not, it's the secret to *Ahavas Yisroel!*"[33]

Yirmi nodded his head slowly in agreement.

"You don't know how many couples have come through this door because of *shalom-bayis* issues. 'He says this' and 'she says that,'" the rav said, mimicking the actual people.

Yirmi smirked.

"And the thing just escalates until some even talk about divorce…after only six months of marriage!"

"And this could change all that?" he asked.

"Not necessarily ALL of it," the rabbi answered. "Some people have more pressing issues than just the way they talk to one another. The book I gave you was not worn out only by me. I've lent it to many couples as well. And when they returned it, they usually happily admitted how mindfulness had greatly and quickly enhanced their communication skills, and therefore their marriage."

As the rosh yeshivah spoke, Yirmi wondered what it would be like after he was married. He had heard his own share of marriage-disaster stories…of people he had thought would be good at marriage but ended up

---

[33] Love of one Jew for another.

not so good. Some worked out the issues on their own, while others ended up in therapy. It was a good thing, he thought to himself, that he was learning the ideas now.

"The improvements to life are endless," said the rosh yeshivah, a sense of awe in his own voice, "whether we're talking about *Mitzvos Bein Adam L'Makom*[34] or *Bein Adam L'Chavero*.[35] It takes work and time to get used to this approach to life, but the rewards are well worth it. People can either not do the work and struggle for the rest of their lives, or they can put in the time at the beginning, and after that find it easier to get what each moment and person has to offer!"

"Well, I'M sold," Yirmi said enthusiastically.

"Of course you are," the rabbi told him. "You're that kind of person already. You just need some fine tuning, and that's happening now."

"Thank God."

"That's why I think you can really help others who aren't so focused. If you can put all this material together into some kind of program and teach it, then God will thank YOU…as well as all those you help!"

Yirmi felt duly complemented but also a bit a bit overwhelmed by the task before him.

---

[34] Between a person and God.

[35] Between one person and another.

"There is still so much I don't understand…"

"But you will, God willing," the rosh yeshivah cut in. Then, looking at his watch, he added, "But it will have to wait for NEXT time. I need to get back to more mundane matters now. We still need to go over the mechanics of the thought process."

Yirmi smiled in anticipation.

It would be difficult for him to wait a WHOLE week before continuing.

THE WEEKS BECAME months and the months, years. TWO of them to be precise. At first he thought that studying the material would interfere with his regular learning, but in the end it didn't. Just the opposite—it enhanced it. And as far as his tefillah was concerned, random thoughts still came from time to time. But he understood them now and was equipped to deal with them patiently and productively.

The biggest change in his life was that he had started teaching. Although he was nervous at first, the more mindful he himself became, the more confidence he gained. He became less afraid of failure and making mistakes because his focus had shifted from success to making the most of each moment. When he slowed down, it became clearer to him that self-imposed pressures did not help AT ALL.

Within the two years of developing and teaching the course, he had become somewhat of an expert on the material, and his name was becoming known. Invitations to present the material came in, and though he was prepared to teach for free, his rosh yeshivah insisted that he accept a fee. It would make the course seem more serious to those he was teaching.

As he walked to the room in which he presented the material at his yeshivah, his OWN small black binder in hand, he was stopped by one of the students.

"Yirmi!" someone called out from several feet behind him.

The voice didn't register at first, because he was going over that day's session in his head as he walked. But then the voice intruded into his thoughts, and he stopped and turned in its direction.

"Ephraim…" he said. "Are you coming today?"

"Wouldn't miss it," he said, approaching and catching his breath.

"Great," Yirmi replied, as they walked together.

"I just wanted to tell you how much of a difference this material has made in my life," Ephraim said.

"I am really happy to hear that."

"I mean, it really made a BIG difference!"

Yirmi stopped to look at him when he realized how emphatic he was.

"In fact," Ephraim continued, "it changed my learning, my dovening…my relationship with God and with people…even with my parents! I'm just so much more aware of how much better I can do things…and WANT to do things because I moved from autopilot to actual pilot!"

Yirmi was deeply moved. He loved making a positive difference in other people's lives, and now he was hearing that he had.

"Boruch Hashem!" Yirmi said. "But I can't take all the credit…I can't even take most of it."

Ephraim wrinkled his brow, not understanding what Yirmi meant.

"Had it not been for the rosh yeshivah," Yirmi explained, "who pushed me to learn about this material and then teach it, I don't think I would have even known about it."

Ephraim's expression turned to one of recognition.

"So," he continued, as they both started walking again, "we have the rosh yeshivah to thank for all this."

As they went through the door, Yirmi was surprised to see that the number of students had basically doubled from the previous week, from 20 students to about 40. Why would they decide to start coming after missing the first three sessions?

No matter, he thought, looking at the clock. It was time to start.

"I realize there are a number of people present today who were not here for the first few sessions. It's a bit of problem, because you missed a lot of important background information that was necessary to get to today's session."

He paused, leaving many wondering if they were going to be asked to leave.

"I would have suggested that you wait until the next cycle," he began, "but I'm going to change that. I'm going to allow everyone to remain, but on one condition: If this is your first session, I ask that you hold back any questions until the end of the class. Unless a question has to do with today's material itself, please write it down and ask me about it later."

Looking around, he saw that everyone seemed comfortable with that.

"Okay," he said, indicating he was ready to start.

"Today we're going to take a deeper look at something we take for granted because it happens so automatically...which is good. We need a certain amount of automation in our thinking. The problem is," he explained, moving from one side of the room to the other to add some interest, "we rely on that automation TOO MUCH...and therefore miss much from life as a result."

He paused for effect. Theatrics were very important, he had come to learn, when getting people to be mindful.

"So let's look at our thought process."

Then he did something that half a year ago would have been completely out of character. He said in his best southern drawl, "Draw!" and immediately jumped into a pose unmistakably that of a gunslinger pulling out his gun and firing it.

No one had any idea what he was talking about. But they were captivated, which was the plan, especially when instead of a gun, he showed a whiteboard marker in his hand. Then returning to himself, he held up the marker up and said more matter-of-factly, "Get it? Draw?"

Smiles filled the room with the odd chuckle here and there, as he turned toward the white board behind him and drew a fancy "E," which he finished decorating as he continued to speak.

"If we're going to learn how to control our thoughts…to live in the present and get the most out of a moment…then we're going to have to understand our thought processes.

"You're probably trying to guess what the big E I drew on the board stands for. Ego? Eccentric? Exit?" he joked.

He scanned the faces and saw people trying to figure it out.

"Essence. This large, elaborate E stands for 'essence'…as in the essence of who you are, which is important to know and understand for obvious reasons. What may be less obvious, and which has stumped many great philosophers and scientists to this very day is WHAT is it? What IS our essence?"

He paused to see if anyone had a suggestion. It wasn't a rhetorical question.

"Anyone? Our essence…what is it?"

It took a few moments, but someone at the back of the room finally blurted out, "Our soul."

"Exactly!" Yirmi said, turning in the direction of the voice.

"So while modern science and psychology grapple with key issues like consciousness and personality, the Torah DEFINITIVELY answers the question. You are, IN ESSENCE, as the famous kabbalist Rabbi Yitzchak Luria explicitly says in Introduction One of Sha'ar HaGilgulim, your soul.

"Now some people have a problem with that. No one has ever seen a soul, so how do we know that one really exists, they ask. The truth is that a soul leaves a footprint…pun intended…every time a person does something contrary to his physical desire, specifically for some higher purpose. Like sharing your sandwich with someone who doesn't have one, even though you REALLY want to eat the whole thing.

"So for those people who have difficulty with the idea of a soul, you can replace 'soul' with 'higher level of consciousness'…which EVERYONE seems to agree we have.

"The only difference between the two," he continued after a brief pause, "is that we're not sure what our higher level of consciousness is…but those of us who KNOW what a soul is will find that to be QUITE helpful in understanding our thought processes, and how to use them to our advantage. We'll come back to that idea later, God willing."

Returning to the white board again, he started to draw something else…but then turned around and said, "You know, I could stand here and try to draw a brain…but I have slides that do a much better job."

Clicking two keys on his laptop, an image immediately appeared on the whiteboard.

"Recognize this?" he asked, as giggles were heard in the background.

"It's your brain. Well, not exactly YOUR brain… because yours probably wears shoes of a different kind."

Slight laughter.

"Mine wears sandals."

Some more giggles.

He waited a moment for the audience to settle down, and then explained, "The brain is what we can call our onboard computer, and it is where thought occurs. Brain and mind, however, are not the same. The brain is part of the visible, tangible world of the body…the physical organ most associated with mind and consciousness. But the mind is not confined to the brain…and it permeates every cell of your body, not just brain cells.

"Traditionally scientists have tried to define the mind as the product of brain activity: The brain is the physical substance and the mind is the conscious product of firing neurons, according to the classical argument. However, increasing evidence shows that the mind goes far beyond the physical workings of the brain, but scientists still CAN'T bring themselves to say SPIRITUAL entity…just yet.

"Thought, also called thinking, is the mental process in which we form psychological associations and models of the world. Thinking is manipulating information, as when we form concepts, engage in problem solving, reason, and make decisions. The act of thinking produces thoughts, and it is THESE thoughts that determine how we experience the world.

"That's a lot of words, I know. But let's break it down into everyday terms. We see that when we have negative thoughts, we view a situation negatively. If we do that often enough, we will earn the inglorious title of pessimist. If we are thinking positively at the time of an experience, we will tend to view it positively…even though someone else may be seeing it negatively, or we ourself may have done so previously.

"How we experience life is fashioned by our current thoughts, from moment to moment. What children learn in their early years has MUCH to say about how they will view the rest of their lives."

He paused to give his listeners a moment to process, while scanning faces for looks of confusion. It was at times like this that he wished he could read minds. Not being able to, he could only ask if anyone had a question. There were a few, so he answered them and continued, as he walked down one aisle of students and back up another. They weren't aware of the tactic, but it was deliberate on his part. He wanted to keep their brains engaged, and movement and change of view were part of doing that.

"This is the question now: Can we control our thoughts?"

He stopped at the front of the room and said with emphasis: "Because if we CAN control our thinking process, then perhaps we can ALSO control how we experience LIFE!"

He paused for effect.

"And THAT is the difference between a MEDI-OCRE life and an amazingly PRODUCTIVE and SUC-CESSFUL life!"

He took a deep breath, and then said, "And WHO doesn't want that?"

"In an article I read in the March 1, 2013, issue of Scientific American, this is what the scientists say:

> We are aware of a tiny fraction of the thinking that goes on in our minds, and we can control only a TINY PART of our conscious thoughts. The vast majority of our thinking efforts goes on sub-consciously. Only one or two of these thoughts are likely to breach into consciousness at a time.

"Hmm," he said, disappointedly. "THAT doesn't sound very promising…I mean, you can't control what you can't access."

"But wait," he said, obviously over-dramatizing. "There's GOOD news! We don't have to control ALL our thoughts…or even MOST of them…to greatly enhance our quality of life!"

He waited to make sure everyone was still following him.

"We just need to control a certain amount of them…mostly the thoughts that affect our self-perception…or the kind of thinking that impacts our mood… or how we evaluate situations…or people.

"Therefore, we need to be aware of the main sources of input that inspire the thoughts we have in any given situation."

He pressed a computer key and the next slide came up.

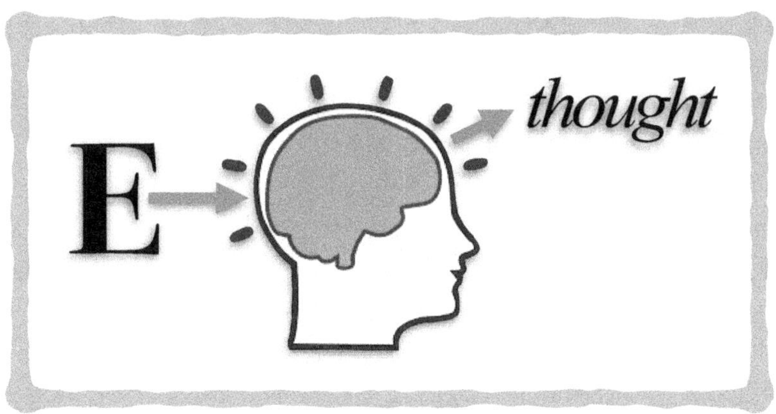

"There is the soul...or higher consciousness. It seems to feed us ideas that result in a certain higher state of consciousness that we all feel, or have felt, from time to time...some more than others. Sometimes we can really notice it breaking through... though some might prefer not to. For example, perhaps I'm considering sharing something that I want for myself. Part of me says to be selfish and keep it all. And part of me says that I should share, because that's the decent thing to do. Any time a brain gets input to do something moral, we can be sure that it came from the soul.

"We can sense the soul's involvement there because of the inner struggle. We can FEEL a sense of selfishness because we're getting INPUT that pushes us in that direction. But we can also FEEL a sense of selflessness, because something is feeding us the idea that it is nobler to share than not to share. If we're getting that message for non-selfish reasons, that's the soul we're hearing. But not if we're sharing for personal gain, perhaps to make someone like us or to do something helpful for us in the future.

"But," he continued, walking around the room again, "there are other times when the soul is talking to our brain and giving us soul-thoughts when we're NOT even conscious of it."

He stopped suddenly, as if he too had just received a sudden message. Then he abruptly turned around and said. "It can really elevate us…bring out the hero in us…you know…make us act so…so non-mundane!"

He checked the faces to see if that reached people. From what he saw, if they didn't already know what he meant, they looked as if they surely wanted to.

"The entertainment industry knows this, and is making trillions of dollars from billions of people by appealing to their messianic side. It's as if we're hard-wired to care about really important things…even more than ourself."

He let people personalize what he was saying.

"We even applaud people who give up their lives for higher causes…wanting to believe that we too would do the same thing if tested.

"Am I right?" he asked.

Heads nodded in agreement, while some people even whispered it to themselves.

"Well, at least I'd LIKE to believe I have it in me to be such a hero…because sometimes I seem to act in ways that strongly suggest just the opposite!"

Some heads nodded in agreement to that as well.

"But there are times when we just dwell on a question. We don't have an answer, or perhaps even a direction to get to an answer. We just mull over the question, wondering about this and wondering about that. Then all of a sudden, an answer comes to us! A light bulb goes off! Where did it come from?

"A lot of times we'll be thinking about some problem…but can't solve it. So we put it aside for the time being for one reason or another…and then later, while not even consciously thinking about the problem, the solution will pop into our head. Where does THAT come from? We might even just wake up with it the next morning. How?

"In fact, sometimes you might just be looking out the window…thinking of nothing specific, but being very relaxed and settled. You might even feel detached from life for the moment, almost like a spectator to the world around you. On one hand, it's very peaceful. On the other hand, all kinds of interesting ideas might go flying through your head, even impressing you…perhaps inspiring you."

"It doesn't happen too often for a lot of people, though people pay good money and try all kinds of ways to increase access to that lofty state of mind. Some methods work better than others, meditation being one of the most popular. But there's something about psychological disembodiment that allows us to access higher states of consciousness and more refined levels of living…if we want to…if we will it…if we learn how to."

He had returned to his starting place behind the lectern, as if to signal the end of the session. He ended by saying, "But clearly that is not how life works for most of us, not MOST of the time anyway. On the contrary, we get all kinds of other thoughts without even trying. Those are the other states of mind we will discuss next session."

He gave a big smile and said, "Hope to see you then, God willing."

Looking at the clock he saw that he was ending five minutes late, though no one seemed to be rushing out. He was already looking forward to the next session. Apparently they were too.

HE SPENT THE first fifteen minutes reviewing the previous session's material, although he usually preferred to have a student do it. When necessary, he would provide a prompt or two, but he felt it was crucial for the students themselves to recall the material for several reasons.

First, it was a signal to them to pay close attention to what was being taught during each class, because the following week someone would have to summarize it. Second, it encouraged them to engage their minds early in the session, which increased their awareness and made them more mindful. And finally, it unwittingly provided valuable feedback, allowing him to gauge how accurately he was being heard and understood.

It had worked well…for the past two years. He himself had come a long way in that time, when he started in a back room of the yeshivah with about ten students. He continued to improve the course, reading new books on the topic, talking to professionals, experimenting on himself.

The rosh yeshivah, still one of his biggest supporters, had been right. Not only did he himself grow from it, not only had he helped many others with the material, but it had definitely become a parnassah. The fact that others were now doing the same thing just about everywhere did not slow down his opportunities to present the material.

The most important change in his life over the two years was his wife, who was now expecting their first child. He met her at one of his presentations at a local shul. Quite ironically, at first neither had considered the other as a potential *shidduch*. That was due to the work of a mutual friend who had known them for years.

It took Yirmi all of three weeks from their first date to decide that he had found his *b'shert*. It took his wife a while longer before she knew. In fact she had seriously considered ending the connection after the third date. It was only after a long intense discussion with the friend and shadchan that she agreed to a fourth date, and she never regretted it. "On the contrary," she told her friend, "I will be forever grateful that you convinced me to go out with him again!"

"There is something called default mode," he now explained to the class of 55 people. "It's this automatic mode…what you might call autopilot…that we just seem to slip into and remain in unless—"

At that point he put one foot on the chair and the other on the desk that he had placed next to the lectern and stood there, to the complete surprise of everyone.

"Unless something happens to wake us up!"

Instantly it became clear what he had intended by the theatrics, and it got a delayed laugh. He kept talking as he carefully made his way back down to ground level.

"If that shocked you a bit, you are probably feeling more alive and more aware at this moment than you were when I just droned on."

He checked faces to see the reactions. He could not tell what everyone was thinking, but he could see enough faces to know that his point had been made.

"My antics caused you…or at least most of you…to shift mental gears. Even though ALL of you physically walked in here today, not ALL of you were present when we started. You were preoccupied with one thing or another, and even though you may have THOUGHT you were paying attention and were in the moment, in truth you weren't—at least not100 percent. You were pretty much in default mode.

"Do you want to hear an amazing statistic? It's astonishing but scary at the same time."

The question was rhetorical.

"Listen to this."

He read each word slowly, carefully, and with a LOT of emphasis. He wanted the information to really have an impact. It was going to be KEY to today's session.

Nearly all your brain's work is conducted in different lobes and regions at the UNCONSCIOUS [sic] level, completely WITHOUT your knowledge. When the processing is done and there is a decision to make or a physical act to perform, that very small job is served up to the conscious mind, which executes the work and then flatters itself that it was in charge all the time. The conscious you, in effect, is like a not terribly bright CEO, whose subordinates do all of the research, draft all of the documents, then lay them out and say, "Sign here, sir." The CEO does—and takes the credit. "The information we perceive in our consciousness is not created by conscious thought… Nor is it reacted to by conscious processes. Consciousness is the middle-man and doesn't do as much work as you think."

"This quote from Time Magazine of June 26, 2015, makes it clear that our brains don't work in a vacuum…something is keeping your two ears apart from each other."

At least HE thought that was funny.

"We happen to live in a very stimulating world with an awful lot going on around us all the time.

"The average person whose eyes are open is always SEEING and sending sight information to the brain, whether you are conscious of this or not. Good OR bad…it all goes in, gets processed, and is added to the incredible data bank inside your brain that has existed from before birth and which has been actively compiling additional information since birth!

"Unlike your eyes—which have to be open to see—your ears are always hearing and your nose is always smelling, triggering all kinds of memories and reactions completely on a subconscious level. If you're sleeping, you might dream about something you're hearing or smelling at the time.

"And of course there are our senses of taste and touch—additional sources of sensory stimulation—which also give our brain input from the outside world. It's a GOOD thing that so much works for us subconsciously. We'd probably go CRAZY having to process and decide about ALL the information bombarding us every single second we're alive!

"Wow!" he said, sitting down as if he had just heard overwhelming news. He wanted everyone to feel the power of what he had been saying.

Then he had an idea. He had tried different tactics in the past, but this one came to him out of the blue, and he smiled. Those who could see him had an expression on their faces that implied, "What's THAT for?"

He abruptly stood up, startling a few people. Turning to one of them, he said, "Good evening…Can I ask your name?"

The young man hesitated for a moment, and then said, "Charlie."

"Charlie?"

"Yes."

"Great," he said, extending his hand to shake Charlie's. "Nice to meet you. Are you enjoying the sessions?"

Charlie thought for a second, and was about to

answer when Yirmi caught him off guard.

"It's okay, Charlie, I was just kidding."

The young man looked relieved not to have to give his opinion in public like that, but was surprised to hear Yirmi say, "I know you are LOVING them!

"Okay, back to business. Here's what I want you to do, Charlie," he continued, as he took him by the arm and gently led him to the front of the room. "I want you to just stand right here, and do nothing but be Charlie...Charlie...?"

"Levy," Charlie finished.

"Charlie Levy," Yirmi repeated before turning to the others and soliciting five more volunteers, which he quickly got.

"Great, thank you. This is only going to take a minute. I just want the five of you to stand directly in front of Charlie, or close to it."

Turning to the one farthest from him, he asked, "And you are?"

"Shmuel."

"Shmuel. Wonderful. Here's what I want you to do, Shmuel. When I tell you to start, I want you to try to convince Charlie to look at something."

"Anything?" Shmuel asked.

"Anything," Yirmi answered. "Are we good?" he asked Shmuel.

"We're good."

"Great."

Moving on to the next person, he was about to ask his name, but was preempted.

"David."

"David, this is your story. I would like you to try to convince Charlie to listen to something when I say start. Copy that?"

"Copy that," David replied with a wry smile.

Yirmi moved to the next person. "Wait!" he said, and placed his hand on his head as if trying to think of something. "Don't tell me…I'm getting it…Your name is…Shaya!" he declared, as if getting the information through some kind of prophecy. "Am I right?"

"I sure hope so," Shaya said. "We've known each other for years already."

"Good point!" Yirmi remarked to chuckles.

"What should I do?" Shaya asked.

"You, my friend, shall try to get Charlie to smell something. And you…" he said, turning to the next person. "Warren." "Warren, you must get Charlie to want to taste something…anything."

"But I don't have anything for him to taste!"

"You don't have to. Just pretend, okay?"

"Okayyyy," Warren said, exaggerating to show he was game.

Turning to the young man closest to him, Yirmi said, "And last, but not least is…"

"Izzz…" the last person joked.

"Izzz…" Yirmi joked back.

"Izzz…Frederick."

"Frederick?"

"Yes…But you can call me Avi."

"Avi sounds more like it."

"Don't tell me," Avi jumped in, "I have to get Charlie to want to feel something."

"Correct," Yirmi confirmed. Then, looking at Charlie, he asked, "Charlie, are you ready for this?"

Charlie made a mock look of concern and said, "I hope so."

"Excellent. Then let's start at 3…2…1…NOW!"

And they did. All five of them at once. Instantly there was a cacophony of sound as each person did his job and tried to get Charlie's attention. It was dizzying. Even Yirmi, who was smiling the whole time, started to get a headache, while others either smiled, laughed, or covered their ears. The experiment was working.

He let them go at it for about three minutes, but when he saw that Charlie was getting overwhelmed, he stopped everyone. "Okay, I think that made the point."

"Which point?" Charlie asked, a semi-serious look of distress on his face. Even the other five looked worn out from the experience.

"Why so much of our brain's function has to be at the subconscious level," Yirmi explained. "The noise everyone created actually DOES occur every day just about all day long. The eyes are constantly sending information to the brain, as are the ears, nose, mouth, sense of touch...and often at the same time. The CONSCIOUS mind is capable of dealing with only so much sensory input at once. For me, just watching a gorgeous sunset can be emotionally overwhelming. When I get bombarded by only TWO sources of information, I can get uptight. My subconscious mind is much better at dealing with all that outside interference...MUCH better."

Turning to the six young men before him, he said, "Thanks, guys. You were perfect," from which they understood they could resume their seats. Then addressing everyone, he continued.

"Thank God for the subconscious mind," Yirmi said with real enthusiasm. "Who KNOWS how many times it has literally saved our necks! I mean, think about it. How many times has it acted like a computer and accomplished so many things for us in the background? And the brain is more sophisticated than any computer!"

"And speaking about the subconscious mind, it is important to point out something. Our subconscious is a source of insights and creativity. It is also the source of random thoughts that tend to be distractions that can take us out of the moment. Both types of thoughts indeed come from our subconscious, in the sense that we are not aware of the origins of these thoughts until we notice that we are having them. But, besides that commonality, they are as different as night and day. The first kind comes from our true essence, our higher self, our souls. The second is a product of the *yetzer-hara*. Although they both come from our subconscious thoughts, they are of a different nature. Part of mindfulness is to recognize this difference in the different unconscious thoughts that enter our mind."

He loved learning and teaching about the brain. It was one of his favorite topics because he believed that the more he understood his own brain, the more he could use it to his advantage.

"But," he observed haltingly, "it has its limitations."

He started to pace back and forth, seeming to speak to himself, although his voice was clearly heard.

"For example I'm praying on Yom Kippur, trying hard to concentrate on the words and my relationship with God…sincerely wanting to make amends for the previous year's mistakes…and all of a sudden, the smell of food makes its way to my nostrils."

He turned to the audience and innocently remarked, "And instead, I start planning my meal for breaking the fast!"

People laughed.

"It kind of cheapens the experience, no?"

People's faces showed they agreed.

"Or I'm learning a page of Talmud…and happen

to overhear something that reminds my brain of a previous experience that just doesn't fit well with the section of Talmud I am currently leaning."

More smiles.

"I think we ALL know what I mean. The subconscious mind can be like an annoying child in the mall who never stops tugging at his parent's hand, constantly saying, 'Let's go here…Let's try that…Let's eat that!' It makes it really hard for the parent to focus on the single task he or she came to do! The world is full of SO much static and is SUCH a distracting place! And we haven't even discussed how our yetzer hara—evil inclination—uses this to its advantage to get us to sin!

"With a MAJOR difference, however," he qualified. "At least with a chatty child you know who is saying what, and how much of it is important and how much is not. That gives the parent the ability to filter out the unimportant stuff and follow through on the mission.

"Not so with the subconscious mind and outside worldly stimulation. The child is external. The subconscious mind is internal. The child has its own voice. The subconscious mind shares ours. That makes it super easy for us to become confused or at least indifferent to what is going on in our brain and what it is making us do or not do.

"If only there were a way to take control and

manage the input of our subconscious mind. We don't want to interfere with the job of our subconscious mind…but we also don't want it to interfere with what should really fall into the realm of conscious mind and choice."

He paced a bit more and gave people some time to think about that. The session was coming to an end, and he wanted everyone to be thinking when they left.

"So that's where mindfulness comes in. This is the importance of self-regulation, which means taking charge of what we think during a moment and how we decide to respond to it. Will our response be up here?" he asked, lifting his hand to indicate a high level, "impacted by our essential being. Or down here?" he continued, dropping his hand as low as it could go without his having to bend over, "subconsciously, on autopilot.

"Fulfillment in life, he concluded, "is up here," raising his hand high in the air again. "A mediocre life at best," he said, lowering his hand once again, "is down here, where tragically so many people live most of their lives.

"All of us are here in this room," Yirmi declared with finality, "because we find that unacceptable."

Facial expressions displayed agreement.

"So let's find a solution together!"

He nodded to indicate he was done.

Slowly and contemplatively, people got up from

their chairs, as if reluctant to leave.

Yirmi just sat down and reviewed the session in his head as he began thinking about the next one.

MANY BOOKS on mindfulness in general had been published, as well as quite a few on JEWISH mindfulness. Every time someone tried to get him to write his own, including his mother, father, and even his wife, Yirmi demurred. "It's a lot of work just to see it sit on the shelf in bookstores," he would tell anyone who raised the subject.

It wasn't until a professional editor who had sat through his presentation TWICE offered to turn his personal notes into a book—and insisted on not being paid—that he begrudgingly agreed. And had the editor not done such a good job with the sample, he might still have refused. But even HE enjoyed reading what the editor wrote, or rather what the editor wrote from what he himself had written.

Now it was his turn. Their system was that the editor would return each chapter of the manuscript for him to proofread and send back. Although he recognized the material as his own, he enjoyed what the editor was doing with it. It was almost magical.

It is amazing how much the outside world—with its various forms of stimuli—affects our way of thinking. Something as simple as a smell can trigger a childhood memory and result in a sense of comfort, or just the opposite.

A person can hear something in the background and revert to another time that evokes an emotional response completely out of step with the current situation. This happens not only when we're awake, but also while we're sleeping. A physical sense receives input from the outside world and sends it to the brain for processing. The result is that it will tell a person what to think and feel.

He took a moment to digest the thought, and experimented while he did. He homed in on what he was seeing, hearing, smelling, etc., and how it was affecting him. He paid attention to what he was touching…the arm of the chair…and what it made him think and feel.

He was amazed that, after all the work he had done so far, he was able to zero in on so much more when he became truly mindful of what was going on around and inside him. It was like breaking through a barrier and sneaking a peek at some other, usually hidden world, although this one was hidden only by a lack of awareness of its existence.

He turned the page and examined the chart that was followed by an explanation:

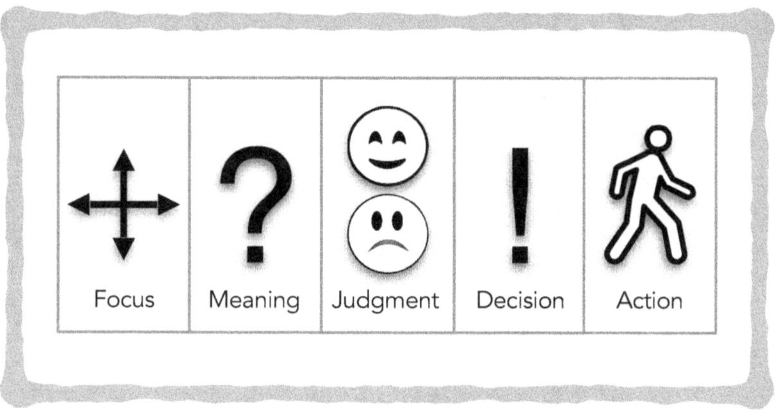

At every single moment you are what you are thinking. So if you want to have any real say over who you are at any given moment, you have to train yourself to be mindful of your thoughts. It's all technique, and mastering it means taking control of your life.

The first thing you have to do is FOCUS…to become aware of your thoughts. Then you can determine the MEANING of those thoughts. Are the thoughts significant and what you want to be thinking now? Yes? Good. No? Then they need to be discarded.

That's the JUDGMENT part of the thought process. So often we judge thoughts from the get-go, before we even know where they came from or why they came. We take for granted that if we are thinking them, the thoughts must belong to us. If they seem appropriate, they reflect us positively to ourself. If they are deemed inappropriate, negativity enters and we automatically feel less secure.

By now it should be clear that thoughts can arise for all kinds of reasons, many subconscious and possibly the result of an outside stimulus that has nothing to do with the person per se. This is especially so when people do not make an effort to tap into their higher selves.

It can be compared to being at a well-attended conference with people of different backgrounds and perspectives. Some will suggest practical ideas while others may say things that just don't make sense. They might even seem ludicrous. In any event, the people in the room will not evaluate themselves by the thoughts of others, but will first consider the ideas and only then judge them.

When it comes to an individual, the conference is internal and therefore quite confusing. The response, however, should be similar. Let the "speaker" say what he insists on sharing, and then judge it. If it is merit-worthy, go with it. If not, push it aside. Then you will be ready for the fourth and fifth steps, DECISION and ACTION.

He liked the way that sounded. It was clear and to the point. All that was missing, he realized, was an example. He inserted the cursor, created a space, and after a few minutes began to type.

For example, David is sitting comfortably and reading a good book when, seemingly out of nowhere, a random thought pops into his head, triggered more than likely by something in the background or something he recently read but didn't pay much attention to. Whatever it was, it got his brain working in a different direction.

At first he didn't really notice. But then he started to feel agitated, and didn't know why. He tried to ignore the feeling, but it was persistent, making it increasingly difficult for him to focus on the words. When he found himself having to reread some sentences several times, he became frustrated. He didn't know what to do.

Then he remembered a book on mindfulness. Although he had skimmed through it, he remembered reading something about this very situation. Putting aside the book he was currently reading, he went to get the mindfulness book.

He sat down with it and quickly flipped through the pages to a chart he remembered seeing. He read the instructions intently and began following them.

"Okay," David said to himself, "First I need to FOCUS on the thoughts I was thinking when the restlessness started."

"That's harder to do AFTER the fact," Yirmi realized. "That means having to recall something you weren't conscious of at the time! It's possible, but increasingly more difficult with each minute that passes." He made a note for himself to be sure to emphasize that point.

He returned to writing.

It took some effort and concentration, but as David considered when he first started feeling edgy, a memory came to him. It was blurry at first, but became increasingly clearer as he focused. To his surprise, he remembered thinking about his first day at yeshivah many years back, which had been an unnerving experience at the time. "So many boys...so large a place...so far from home..." he found himself recalling out loud.

As he thought about that long-ago day, the

feeling he had while reading returned and overtook him, really surprising him. "Where did THAT come from?" he wondered aloud. He picked up the original book to see what might have triggered the distant memory and the feeling of anxiety from over a decade ago.

Scanning the pages, he knew he had found it when his emotions suddenly responded. It was as if he had opened an old wound! HE, the present David, had casually read about the old yeshivos of Europe and the learning conditions at that time. But it somehow woke up the past David when his brain translated the information into a personal experience, triggering the memory which triggered the feeling.

"Wowwww," David intoned to himself, putting down the book to contemplate what he had just grasped. He found himself absolutely amazed at how his brain did all THAT...and on its OWN too...without checking with him, so to speak.

He snapped out of his moment of wonder and thought, "Okay, what next?" He continued to read.

"Do these thoughts have any MEANING for me?"

He thought about it. His automatic response was "not at all." But then he wondered if his brain were sending him some kind of subconscious message that he should pay attention to. He had read that the subconscious mind has saved people's lives that way…However, he couldn't find any hints after considering for a few minutes and moved to the next step.

"JUDGMENT," he read. "You have to assess the importance or lack thereof of the thought, and how it should help decide your future course of action. Subconscious thoughts that emanate from your higher self…your soul…are worthy of our attention and energy. Random subconscious thoughts that our brains happen to throw at us need to be ignored. Judgment distinguishes between the two types of subconscious thoughts so that we can meaningfully move forward."

"Well," David pondered, "given that the thought was simply some random memory triggering an inconvenient and inappropriate reaction, I'd say that the best thing would be to go to the fourth step, DECISION, and leave the past behind me…where it belongs…go back to my book…and live in the present!"

His eyes returned to the book and he saw that the fifth step was called ACTION, so that's exactly what he took. He put the mindfulness book on the shelf for another time and calmly went to the chair he had been sitting on. He picked up the book he had been reading when all this started, found where he left off, made himself comfortable, and began to read.

Thoughts still came to him, triggered by one thing or another, but none of them distracted him for very long. He would think to himself something like "not now" or "not important," and the thoughts would vanish into thin air.

About half an hour later he glanced at his watch and realized that it was time to go. He inserted a bookmark and put down the book, realizing how enjoyable those last 30 minutes of reading had been.

"Hey, this stuff really works!" he said out loud. As he got up and moved on, he focused on the five steps to controlled thinking. He wanted to remember them well…for the rest of his thoughtful life!

Yirmi went back and reread what he had written. He tweaked it a bit and, satisfied that he had made his point, he too moved on.

Here's what's important. Everyone wants to live a QUALITY life. Who doesn't want to leave this world knowing that he got as much as possible from his life? And as we already learned, that includes both easy times and hard times, highs and lows, successes and failures. No one can control all that and have a PERFECT life.

Unless, that is, we define "perfect" a different way. Instead of saying that perfection means we avoid all the snags—which we can't—it means that we deal with something in a mature and meaningful way. Perfect means that life gave us opportunities to go in one direction or another, to respond to situations on autopilot or to wake up and realize that we have a choice about how we respond by being mindful of each opportunity.

We've seen the results, sometimes on purpose, sometimes accidentally. On occasion we've been super-FOCUSED, totally aware of what was going on around us. We were completely conscious of what life was throwing our way, what the opportunity of the moment was. It allowed us to be sharper, clearer about our goals, and decisive in action. And it felt good and calm to be in control, impressed by our ability to think and act on a higher plane, in a more sophisticated state of mind.

We are inclined to greatly underestimate ourself, because society—from which we learn so much about life and who we're supposed to be—underestimates us. There is a whole other self to us, our ESSENTIAL self, that is just waiting to be tapped into so it can guide us. It is anything but random. It's not like memories that are waiting to interrupt our moments, to make us worry about the future or fret about the past. It is ETERNAL and only exists in the moment.

Call it your higher level of consciousness, or call it your soul, which is its REAL name. Either way, it is a VERY powerful source of information…even a mystical one. What is more significant is that is a VERY important source of direction. It's always there and always talking. But it does so in a mature, calm way, which is why it so often gets drowned out by the louder, more insistent voices.

To tap into our higher self usually requires a CONSCIOUS act on our part. On occasion it can happen automatically if the circumstances are right, such as when we're acutely mindful or doing something extremely meaningful. Just seeing an awesome sight—like a beautiful and majestic sunset or something similarly spectacular—can silence all the extraneous voices and allow the higher consciousness to speak its mind.

Such moments have changed people, sometimes only temporarily, sometimes permanently. The higher voice has the power to elevate us in the moment and leave us on a different intellectual and emotional plane, in a higher state of mind. It is one of the most calming and uplifting feelings we can have in life.

But everyday life doesn't give us many awesome moments…at least those that we notice with our everyday eyes. Life's distractions vie for our senses, forcing us to settle for a less conscious level of living. That is the way a vast majority of people have lived since we first left the Garden of Eden.

But if we train ourself to look at life differently, then life will look different to us. Many people are only happy when life makes them happy, and are sad when it doesn't. A mindful person is able to control his state of mind, and that is the secret to a continuously happy life, because he can filter out detrimental ideas and stimuli.

He stopped at that point. He felt that the chapter had a natural ending there, not to mention that he could use a break. He thanked God for everything. As he leaned back and sipped coffee, he reminisced about the beginning of his journey years previously and where it had led him.

But apparently he wasn't finished yet. He had a good friend to whom he liked to send what he had written for feedback. This friend was also interested in the connection between mindfulness and Torah, and often provided important comments that helped him tweak what he had written.

A few days passed and Yirmi had moved on to the next chapter when the phone rang. It was his friend, who said, "I really like what you wrote, and especially the model you used. But I think you made a jump to using the five criteria as a tool to observe and evaluate thoughts. It seems to me there is a point to be made prior to that."

"Namely?" Yirmi asked, intrigued.

"That even the events that happen to us outside our thoughts only have meaning based on how we think about them, in terms of the criteria."

"What do you mean?" Yirmi encouraged him, happy to get the feedback.

"If something happens, its impact on us will depend on whether or not we choose to focus on it. This will affect the meaning of the event for us, how we feel about it, and what we decide to do."

"Very true."

"In other words, and this is worth stressing, it is these thought processes that shape and determine our life experience—NOT the events themselves. It is a really important insight that most people don't realize...that our WHOLE experience is shaped by our OWN thinking!"

"An example would probably be helpful with this."

"I have one. Back in the spring of 2009 a novel influenza A (H1N1) virus emerged. It was detected first in the United States and spread quickly across the country and around the world. This new H1N1 virus contained a unique combination of influenza genes not previously identified in animals or people."

"I remember."

"In the office where I work, some people couldn't stop talking about it while others didn't want to hear anything about it. In the end no one in the office got it, thank God. But the quality of life of the people who chose NOT to worry was certainly better than the people who chose to focus on it. The latter worried a lot, kept checking websites to see the latest on the breakout, and lost a great deal of work time along the way."

"I see what you mean," Yirmi said, incorporating it into his own thinking. "A person could ask himself, 'Am I obsessed with it or am I able to focus on family, friends, Torah, God? What aspect of the situation am I focused on? What meaning and insights can I take away from it? How am I judging what is happening? What am I going to do about it? Perhaps I could help someone else or make some changes to my life."

"Exactly!" was my friends response. "And depending on the answers, each person's experience of the crisis will be different."

"That's excellent! Thanks.

But he wasn't finished yet. "A corollary of this is that since focus, meaning, etc. are thought processes, it follows that the nature and quality of our thinking will shape how we experience life. Mindful thinking will cause life to be experienced differently from when thoughts just occur randomly. We need to notice our thinking and then separate our true identity from the content of our thoughts. You know that we are not our thoughts, as we've discussed a number of times."

"For sure."

"THIS," my friend added, "gets us to the level you mentioned here, namely that we can apply the five disciplines of focus, meaning, etc. to our thoughts themselves as well, not purely to outside events that occur."

"I get it. That's good."

"And while we're on this topic, you should probably make it clear that you don't limit 'meaning' to the thought being meaningful in a DEEPER sense, but also in the PLAIN sense…as applied to outside events especially…for example, 'What is the meaning of what I am observing or experiencing?'

There was a moment of silence as Yirmi finished taking notes while his friend patiently waited. Finally Yirmi said, "I think I got all that…which was great, as always. Thank you SO much for taking the time to read the material and discuss your ideas and corrections. It helps make the book much more accurate."

"Thanks for the opportunity," my friend said, and after a few more niceties we said goodbye.

Thank God, Yirmi thought to himself, that he had such a friend…and a rosh yeshivah, for that matter, who had not only picked up on what he was feeling when he was much younger, but who also understood such feelings and had the foresight to encourage him to learn about them and teach the material that was now making its way into book form.

He reflected on other times that Divine Providence had been leading him during his life. How much more was there that he didn't even know about or recognize? We are inclined to just live from moment to moment, he thought, like boats on a moving stream, flowing with whatever current there is. It's God Who is guiding us, and if we pay attention, we can be more a part of our growth process and not simply a product—and in some cases a victim—of it.

That thought stayed with him until his body sent him strong hints to get some rest. He agreed with the thought and did exactly that.

THE ROOM WAS half empty, but Yirmi wasn't surprised. He had completed the first part of the course, and in the last session had informed the participants that the next two classes would be on "Torah Mindfulness." He didn't expect that subject to be popular with the masses, and was actually grateful to have the number of people that he did.

"Thanks for coming back for the second part of the series," Yirmi began.

"Thanks for continuing them!" someone called back. Others nodded in agreement, and Yirmi responded, "I appreciate that.

"In fact," he continued, as he reached into a large box next to him on the desk and pulled out a big red pillow in the shape of a heart for everyone to see, "appreciation is hugely important for mindfulness… and as a measure of it."

Then he tossed the pillow to someone in the front row, with a motion slow enough for him to instinctively catch it. He smiled to signal that it was just in good fun.

"Dovid *HaMelech* wrote in Tehillim 51:19, 'The sacrifices of God are a broken spirit; God, You will not despise a broken and crushed heart.'"

Hands in pockets, he walked over to the window and looked up at the sky. As he did, some birds flew by with such grace that it made him feel awe.

"It sounds as if Dovid *HaMelech* is telling us that God is only happy with us if we walk around brokenhearted…humbled to the point of a broken spirit."

He paused for a moment, and turning to his audience, he continued.

"I can understand a contrite spirit…humility is the essence of being a good *eved Hashem*—servant of God. But why must my heart and spirit be broken before I am on a par with a desired sacrifice?"

There was silence for a moment, so he continued.

"The question isn't rhetorical, so I welcome your suggestions."

By the looks of it, no one had realized that he was actually asking THEM to answer the question. This was evident from the way they now seemed to change their posture in order to go into thinking mode.

He gave them about half a minute to come up with ideas, and when none were forthcoming, he strategized how to pull an answer from them.

"Well let me ask you this..." he started, pacing again. "I'm assuming that everyone here observes the mitzvos on some level...but the truth is that even if we don't, we've surely done good deeds at some point in our life. So here's the question: Have you felt CHANGED by that...even momentarily?"

He stopped and faced them.

"I mean, you know, different. Elevated. On a higher plane. Feeling extra joy at being you. More ALIVE, perhaps, even AWED by a simple action."

People seemed to be thinking about it, and by the looks on some of the faces, they knew exactly what he was talking about.

"It actually amazes me," he told them, "it really does. I even made a kind of personal study of it...why I felt so great just by helping someone for a moment...unexpectedly...especially when I could have avoided the opportunity but didn't. I thought to myself, 'If such acts make me feel so good about myself and life, why don't I take advantage of all those that come my way?'"

There was some head nodding.

"Was it the spontaneity that made it so nice? Or the way I overcame my yetzer hara and did the right thing that made me feel so good? I found that it was that, but also something else. Something far more profound and promising.

"You see, some people look at Torah mitzvos only as obligations that test our loyalty to God. The more you do, the more loyal you are to God. The better you do them, the more loyal you are to God."

He started walking as he continued talking.

"That's true…to some degree. But there's more. What more? Well, for some, it is a matter of tikun—which is the kabbalistic word for rectification—tikun of the person and, ultimately, tikun of the world…and that's definitely true. But there is MORE still, and it is that more that helped me understand at least a little bit better what God was giving us through Torah."

He slowly and deliberately went back to the lectern, purposely doing it in such a way that the participants would follow his every move. Then he leaned forward over it, to make the moment more intimate. He wanted to draw them in before making his next point.

"Words are interesting conventions, aren't they? Some of the smaller ones, by their inclusion or exclusion, can completely change a thought…perhaps even cause a better or worse consequence. It happens to writers all the time. Someone means to write, 'The man did not steal the diamond,' but accidentally leaving out the word "not," he writes instead, 'The man

DID steal the diamond,' and makes an innocent man guilty just like that!"

"Not every editor catches every mistake either, which, as a writer, I have found to my chagrin.

"But then you have a word like 'mindfulness.' An interesting word…one that I don't think I even heard for the first part of my life. How about you?"

Some people took it as a rhetorical question and just waited for what was coming next, while others shook their heads.

"If you think about it, it almost seems silly. You have to make a big thing about paying attention to life? Shouldn't it just be something that we do automatically?"

This time heads nodded "yes."

"But then again," he said, "think of all the accidents that have happened just on the roads alone… because some people failed to pay attention to the right thing at the right time! There are people sitting in jail today for manslaughter because they were using their phones while driving a car, and killed someone as a result!"

"Tragic…" he said trailing off, as if the idea struck a personal chord.

Then he snapped back to reality.

"Who is the number one enemy of God and the Jewish people?"

Without hesitation, several people called out the

same answer, "Amalek."

"Amalek. That's correct. Amalek," he said, walking once again, "that nasty nation that attacked us on our way out of Egypt, and cooled us down! Amalek, that presumptuous nation that attacked and murdered children of God to open the door to future attacks by other nations! AMALEK!" he deliberately said in a louder, dramatic voice, then more quietly, "that destructive descendant of Eisav that has done more over the millennia to undermine belief in God than any other people!"

He stopped, and looked piercingly at his audience, who followed his every word.

"How? HOW was it done? How Is it done now? Because make no mistake about it: Amalek is alive and well today, destroying mankind the same way it ALWAYS has, whether a single group of people or individuals who have bought into the gospel of Amalek and become merchants for it!"

He paused, purely for effect.

"How does Amalek do it? What is the secret to Amalek's success, if you can even call it that?…What is the weapon of choice?"

If anyone knew the answer, it wasn't being volunteered. Some weren't even sure what he meant by Amalek today.

"One word," he said turning to the white board behind him and writing in big block letters as he slowly sounded them out:

D…I…S…T…R…A…C…T…I…O…N.

"We're first introduced to Amalek in the Torah as a nation, but the Zohar makes it clear that Amalek the 'spirit' existed long before Amalek the people did, as pointed out in *Ki Seitzei* 281b. Everything in the physical world has its root in the spiritual world, and the PEOPLE of Amalek, based on their approach to life, became the perfect VESSEL for the 'soul' of Amalek.

"Therefore, even though Amalek the people died out, Amalek the spirit goes on and WILL go on until the end of history…until Moshiach comes and vanquishes it by paving the way for the ultimate revelation of God…it should happen already in our time!"

Some *"amens"* were quietly heard around the room.

"Amalek is a series of classes on its own. For the time being though, the only part of the discussion that concerns us for now is its methodology for keeping us from connecting to God, its main goal of goals.

"And make no mistake about it. Being disconnected from GOD and being disconnected from LIFE are the same thing, as the Torah says in *Devarim* 4:4, 'You who cleave to God, your God, are alive, all of you, this day.'

"People who are out of touch with God are out of

touch with life, no matter how alive they might say they feel, even smiling while they say it. There is living and there is living, and this is what the Torah means by *Devarim* 30:19: 'This day I call on the heaven and the earth as witnesses [that I have warned] you: I have set before you life and death, the blessing and the curse. CHOOSE LIFE, so that you and your offspring will LIVE.'

"Amalek is the antithesis of mindfulness, hence the language of mikreh—chance. Thus the *Aleph* of kisay in *Shemos* 17:6 and the Aleph of vayikra represent mindfulness…the opposite of Amalek. Amalek can use random thoughts—which are just random memories stored in the brain for future use and triggered by current thoughts and emotions—to distract a person from the spiritual potential in the moment.

"That is why God takes Amalek's attack so personally in the Torah, even going to war against it in whatever form it takes, until the end of Amalek's existence altogether! Interrupting a person's relationship with God is a capital offense as far as heaven is concerned…worthy of divine retribution."

He took a deep, contemplative breath at that moment, and made a facial expression that indicated how difficult the task was.

"Its greatest weapon against the service of God is not some powerful nuclear bomb, or some high-tech laser…or any of the conventional or psychological weapons. Its greatest weapon is DISTRACTION…making sure that at that crucial moment when you want to use a mitzvah to emotionally reach out to God, you reach out emotionally to something else instead."

He gave everyone a minute or two to contemplate that.

"Amalek might use fear to distract us…or just some curious noise…or a hungry stomach…or a friendly voice…or any number of things that have the POWER to tear our concentration away from the God-connecting meaning of what we're doing…just at the crucial moment, so that we miss our connection and stay on the same or lower spiritual plane than we are supposed to be on.

"Such moments are incredibly important to our spiritual growth, but also so fleeting that most people don't even notice what they are losing along the way. And as Amalek knows, if it happens often enough, people will spiritually stagnate and feel less emotionally connected to God than they otherwise would be. They'll backslide spiritually, and eventually accept a lower level of spiritual life, missing out on everything that is truly important, not only in THIS world, but especially in the NEXT one."

He paused to collect his thoughts, and to let everyone else catch up.

"In a nutshell," he summed up, "Amalek is ANTI-MINDFULNESS. And you know why? Because it knows that if we take the time to pay attention to reality through the eyes of our soul, we will become sure about God and His Torah…And nothing pushes away the spiritual blackness of Amalek MORE than spiritual clarity.

"In essence, this is what the Rambam was telling us when he answered his own question about how to come to love and fear God. He said in *Yad Chazakah, Yesodei HaTorah*, 2:2, and I quote…" at which point he picked up a piece of paper and read, "'When one contemplates His actions and His wondrous and great creations and sees in them His wisdom, that it has no limit and no end, IMMEDIATELY he will love and praise Him, and desire tremendously to know His great Name.'

"The Rambam speaks about contemplation… which is the ESSENCE of mindfulness. And since this is the exact OPPOSITE of what Amalek wants, then you can take this as the Rambam's way of telling you how to best arm yourself against so formidable an enemy…that has been able to vanquish great minds over the millennia, turning them into atheists and agnostics and accomplices in its war against God!"

"Yeah, like my brother!" a voice called out, stopping Yirmi in his tracks. It didn't take long for all eyes to focus on the source of the voice, which made the person regret he had said anything. Too late.

Instead of showing his regret, he instead elaborated.

"My brother," the young man boldly began, "is not the type to do what the Rambam just spoke about —rather what we just heard he spoke about. He's never been the contemplative type, but is usually interested in the more material aspects of life. He's more of a what-you-see-is-what-you-get kind of guy. He never cared about taking the time to understand how we know God exists and that Torah is from Sinai."

By the expressions of others in the room, they too had to deal with similar people in their own circles.

"As he grew older, he became more attracted to a secular lifestyle…or should I say, DISTRACTED by it. We used to have these discussions at first…actual arguments…where I'd try to point out the mistakes in his thinking. But he would just argue back, quoting THIS scientist or THAT professor. I even took the time to look up what they said, so I could point out the fallacies in their points of view, but he grew tired and frustrated with me, and then would hang up the receiver, so to speak, telling me that I was too naive to understand or accept what he did."

Yirmi had a sad look on his face. He sympathized and empathized as well. He also had a close friend who did the same thing years back, and he had been powerless to halt the journey away from Torah. The discussion opened an old wound.

"We don't speak that much these days," the

young man continued. "He got his MBA and is seemingly content leading his completely secular lifestyle. I basically see him only at family simchas…where he is usually trying to convince some unsuspecting relative or friend of the truth of his way of life! Unfortunately he has given up on me and, I have to admit, I have also given up on him."

The room went completely silent at that point. Even the birds outside seemed to have stopped chirping.

After what seemed like half an hour, but which had only been a few minutes, Yirmi felt the need to encourage the speaker and anyone else who was dealing with similar disappointments.

"Listen," he said, "bigger miracles have happened. I think we've all seen some of them. But I really appreciate your sharing that personal story with us. It helps to make the point, showing how Amalek is able to use our weaknesses against us…to get our attention away from what we should be attending to…all the while weakening us spiritually…until we fall under its control.

"It reminds me of a story told about the Chofetz Chaim…how on waking early one morning he was confronted by his yetzer hara, which said,

'You're a tired, old man. Surely after all those years of rising early, you can sleep in ONE morning.' But the Chofetz Chaim wasn't fooled and answered, 'If

YOU'RE up this early in the morning, there's no reason why I shouldn't be.'"

There was subtle laughter.

"Now the Chofetz Chaim obviously did not think he was talking to another entity, at least not one OUTSIDE himself. Rather his age and tiredness made him feel like sleeping a little later…as if being convinced by an inner voice. But the Chofetz Chaim—being the Chofetz Chaim—realized where that voice originated, and was therefore able to respond to it in kind, with his love of God and His *mitzvos*."

"That is the POWER of Torah," Yirmi said, stealing a glance at the clock. Wow! Time had gone by so quickly! "The power is mindfulness. From the moment we wake up in the morning and thank God for returning our soul, after which we wash with *negel vasser*—night water—to get rid of the spiritual impurity that comes from sleep…to the moment we go to bed at night after saying the *Shema* and *Hamapil*, blessings before sleep, we have *mitzvos* and *mitzvah*-like activities that, if we take them seriously, MAKE us pay attention to each moment and the opportunity it presents.

"For example, every normal weekday morning I have to put on *tefillin*…or phylacteries, according to some…"

That got some smiles.

"Now, I can choose to space out while I execute this phenomenal directive which is so incredibly kab-

balistic and which has such potential to rectify me…
and the world beyond me…to such an extent that
some great people in the past who understood all this
used to shake uncontrollably while putting on their
tefillin…"

"Phylacteries!" someone jokingly called out, making people chuckle and Yirmi smile.

"The point is that if I just use this 'unusual' activity
to draw me into the moment so that I'm being completely absorbed by it, then my quality-of-life meter
shoots up, WAY up. The more mindful I become of the
mitzvah, understanding what it is, how to do it, what
each of the parts is meant to do for me and the world
—you get the picture."

He scanned the faces to make sure they did.

"In fact," he said building to a climax, "a mitzvah…if appreciated and used properly…is a PORTAL
to the moment."

He paid attention to their expressions as he said
that and was pleased to see that the idea resonated
with at least most of them.

"That's a beautiful idea," a man said from the
middle of the room. He looked about 60, and reli-
giously well seasoned.

"I agree," Yirmi said.

"First of all, I want to commend you on your series of shiurim."

"Thank you very much," Yirmi said, somewhat taken aback by the unexpected compliment.

"Clearly you put a lot of thought into the material, which I have found most uplifting."

Yirmi smiled his appreciation this time.

"But this last class, I have to say, has been the most inspiring of them all, for me at least."

"I'm really happy to hear that. That was my goal…to inspire."

"Well, I think my fellow classmates will agree with me when I say that you have succeeded."

Heads nodded in agreement, and Yirmi acknowledged them.

"This idea of Torah and mitzvos being a portal into the moment in which you do them," the man continued, "really struck me."

"How so?" Yirmi asked.

The man smiled a knowing grin, and then began to explain.

"Because it answered a question that I have had for the last 45 years!"

"Do you mind sharing that question with the rest of us?"

"Not at all," the man said. "It's important to me that I do."

"The floor is all yours," Yirmi said, sitting down on the chair next to the lectern.

"When I was just a bochur," the man began, clearly emotional, "I had this rebi in yeshivah ketanah.

He must have been about 45 years old at the time. Unfortunately, he passed away about two years ago…"

His voice trailed off, as he was apparently warding off some deep emotions. Then, collecting himself, he continued.

"It didn't take long for me to respect and value this teacher of mine. From the beginning there was always something special about him…and the way he taught…especially by example. He was, what they might say in parts of the world, the real deal."

Yirmi knew what he meant, but he let the man say it in his own words.

"He was always *b'simchah*…no matter what."

It was clear the man was reliving his memories and feelings as he spoke…so great was the man he was speaking about.

"Even when he mourned the loss of his parents, I recall, you could feel his great loss, and sorrow…and yet still sense his *simchas hachaim*."

"Joy of life," Yirmi translated for those who might not have been familiar with the term.

"Yes," the man said. "If anyone lived in the moment, it was my rebi…If something ever bothered him, you wouldn't know, because he never showed it on the outside. He didn't want to waste a single moment of life, and you felt the same way in his presence.

"When he walked into a room, you could feel the

energy. It just lifted you…no matter WHAT you were feeling at the time."

The man thought for a moment, and everyone waited for him. They too were enjoying the memories.

Finally he said, "But I never knew to what to ascribe his obvious joy and sense of well-being until you spoke of using a *mitzvah* as a portal to the moment. If anyone lived in the moment, it was my rebi…"

"Rav Boruch?" another voice said from the other side of the room. "Rav Boruch Mueller?"

The man turned sharply in surprise and recognition. "Yes! How do you know?" he asked, turning toward the voice.

"Because your description fits only one man I know, and that was my rebi!"

The first scrutinized the second to see if he remembered him. Something about him seemed familiar, but he wasn't sure.

"When were you at the yeshivah?" he asked the man who interrupted him.

"Early eighties."

"REALLY? That's when I was there!"

He looked even more intently, trying to recall the face. Realizing he was having trouble, the second man identified himself: "Yosef Shapiro."

The name didn't ring a bell at first, but then the first man's face changed from one of confusion to surprise.

"Yosef SHAPIRO?" he asked, obviously incredulous. "That's YOU?"

"In person..." Mr. Shapiro confirmed.

"Wow..." he said, sincerely amazed. "I guess 40 years is a LONG time. Binyomin..." added, starting to introduce himself.

"Horowitz," the man completed. "I didn't recognize you at first, but once you started speaking, I remembered your voice."

"You have a good memory," Binyomin told him.

"Not always these days," he confessed. "But you are one person who is hard to forget."

His lifted eyebrows said, "What do you mean?"

Yosef continued, "You were...what they call...I guess...the teacher's pet!"

It was 40 years later, but words are keys to memories and their emotions, and Binyomin found himself blushing.

"I just could not get enough of our rebi," he confessed, and I guess I overdid it somewhat,"

"Overdid it?" Shapiro said. "We were JEALOUS of your devotion...not only at the time...but even years later. As you can see today, you were able to receive and absorb something that every one of us who knew the rav would have loved to carry within us the rest of our life. The moment to do that existed, and you used it properly. We didn't take it as seriously as you did. To quote the rav," he said, looking at Yirmi, which made him feel awkward, being half his age and certainly having half his knowledge, "we did not MIND the MOMENT."

Everyone seemed to be enjoying this turn of events, but time was running out. So Yirmi used the spontaneous reunion as a way to end the session.

"Gentlemen," he said, and everyone looked at him. "This WAS an unexpected surprise…actually MOMENT, REAL *Hashgochah Pratis*…Divine Providence. I'm sure I don't have to suggest to the two of you to follow up after today's sessions, but I…or rather, WE…" he said, looking at faces for agreement, "thank you for sharing your memories of an obviously great man and example, and for really pulling us into THIS moment."

He gave people time to consider what he said.

"I looked around the room as you spoke, and from what I saw, I'd say you had the attention AND emotions of everyone in the room. I know you certainly had MINE. Your experiences, as little as we know about them, were portals to THIS moment, and it was really ENLIGHTENING…inspiring."

Both men were touched by his words.

He gave that last thought a bit of time so as to not undermine its importance or effect. And then he brought the session to an end.

"This is obviously just the beginning of a much longer and deeper discussion about how the Torah, the learning of Torah, and the *mitzvos* promote mindfulness. Give it some thought, and if you have any ideas or questions, we can devote a session to them AFTER the next one...the last official session in this series of classes, Mindfulness, Torah, and Redemption."

There were smiles of anticipation on some faces.

"Thank you as always for coming and being part of the program. I look forward to seeing you next time. Shalom."

As Yirmi turned to the lectern to collect his things, some students approached to ask questions. In the meantime Binyomin Horowitz and Yosef Shapiro found one another, shook hands, and swapped cell numbers. They recounted a few more memories of good days long gone and agreed to get together to share more.

Yirmi saw them across the room and was really happy for them. But then he realized he was noticing them while listening to the question of someone else, and that wasn't very mindful of him. Consciously intensifying his concentration, he gave the student in front of him his undivided attention, and the moment came alive for him as well.

HIS WIFE LOOKED over the curriculum while she sat at the kitchen table, having a well-earned coffee. She had spent most of the morning getting the children ready for cheder and gan, rarely a smooth process even WITH her husband's help.

He amazed her when she had time to think about it. Each morning without fail he rose early so before dovening he could get in some learning while the world was still dark and quiet. Then he dovened at *neitz*[36] before learning a bit more and returning home

---

[36] Sunrise. A *Neitz Minyan* begins the *Shemoneh Esrai* exactly at the *halachically* calculated time of sunrise, which of course changes each day.

to help with the children. And even though he insisted that his daily nap made it all possible, she was adamant that he did not get enough sleep.

It was at that time that he would usually remind her of how little sleep SHE got and how tiring her life had to be, juggling the family with her own ongoing learning, tehillim, etc. He got tired, he would tell her, just THINKING about all the things SHE did each day. They would settle for mutual admiration.

It wasn't always that way, she would tell others who came to her for help with shalom bayis.[37] Like many young couples, which they still were, they had their squabbles. There were good weeks and not so good weeks. "What changed?" people always asked.

"Mindfulness" was the answer.

As Miri's husband became increasingly more involved in the whole idea of mindfulness, their relationship increasingly improved. Yes, she was suspicious at first. Was the change permanent? Or just a temporary upgrade. Four years later, she could testify to the former, and she was grateful for it every day.

So many arguments and fights between people, especially between husbands and wives, are spontaneous. One partner starts with a comment that on that particular day, at that time, and in that way triggers

---

[37] Peace in the house, usually but not exclusively referring to the level of cooperation between husband and wife.

some kind of negative emotion in the other, who then feels a strong need for self-defense.

This doesn't always happen in the most diplomatic way possible, thus triggering a counter-defense. It doesn't take long for the couple to sling terrible things at one another as if they were mortal enemies.

If it happens often enough, it starts to erode the positive feelings that existed. It is amazing how many marriages—and relationships in general—disintegrate because the partners don't think twice before using hurtful words and damaging remarks that become like self-fulfilling prophecies. The marriage didn't have to fall apart, but it did after the couple accidentally said things that led in that direction.

"In any case," Rebbetzin Miri—as some began to call her much to her chagrin—once told a friend, "everything changed the day Yirmi took a few extra moments to consider his response to something I probably shouldn't have said anyway." Her voice had a sound of mischievousness in it.

"What did you say?" the friend asked.

"It's not important," she answered. "What is important is that rather than quickly defend himself, he first asked himself what he SHOULD say."

"So what did he say?" asked her friend, unable to hold back her curiosity.

"Actually nothing," the rebbetzin answered. "He just sat there with a sympathetic look on his face that made me forget why I was upset in the first place!"

Miri could see her friend retreat into her own mind and memory, as if checking her personal situation against the one she had just heard about. Squabbles were not uncommon in her house…but they usually ended with one or both of them going to another room, leaving the disagreement unresolved…again.

"Nothing?" the friend finally asked.

Miri thought for a moment. "Well, nothing at first. But then he finally said something like 'I never realized how much that bothered you.' Then he corrected himself. 'No, I DID know how much it bothered you. But when you would confront me about it, MY feelings usually got hurt, so I defended myself rather than apologize. This time, however, I waited, and when I didn't respond immediately, my initial thoughts and feelings had time to move on…and then the most amazing thing happened! I calmed down and began to hear YOU…instead of ME…and I actually felt bad for YOU, and not for ME. It's…it's so…REDEEMING!'"

Needless to say, her friend was impressed, as were all the other women she had mentioned it to over the years.

"So you never disagree?" one newly married young woman once asked, obviously incredulous.

Miri had laughed. "No," she replied. "We still disagree plenty. Otherwise it would be TOO perfect a marriage, and no one has that! The difference is that when we do have different opinions about something, Yirmi and I no longer react quickly and impulsively. We agreed to take a minute or two before responding, and those short moments mean SO much to years of shalom bayis!"

Now, as she sat at the kitchen table, enjoying her coffee and looking at her husband's course outline, she noticed that the venue for the final session was different. Rather than returning to the same lecture room, it was scheduled to take place outdoors…in a camping spot off a country road not too far from their home, and she asked her husband about it.

"Why the change of location?"

He smiled to himself as he slipped his laptop into its bag.

"Redemption."

"Redemption?"

She knew that whenever he gave her a cryptic answer, he wanted her to ask more…as if the answer required the drama to be fully appreciated. Sometimes for the fun of it, she pretended not to want to know, and just left him hanging. But she knew that he was aware of her game, and she wasn't up to playing it now.

"What redemption?"

"Well," he explained as he put the rest of his things into the computer bag, "this final lesson is about mindfulness and redemption, so I thought it would be more effective to redeem them from the four walls of the classroom they've been coming to for weeks already. You know, change of pace, change of perspective."

"Nice. But you're meeting outdoors? What if someone has an allergy or something?" she asked.

"Good point," he acknowledged. "That's why we ask a variety of questions on the application form, and I chose the location based on the composition of this group."

"Hmm..." she said, going back to reading the outline.

"Besides," he added, "I made sure to pack plenty of tissues just in case someone missed that question or has an allergy he didn't previously know about."

"Wise," she commented, continuing to read, and then said, "This point you've never mentioned before."

"Which?" he asked, tightening his tie and putting on his jacket.

"How the 10 plagues were a way of drawing them into the moment as a means to redemption."

He stopped to reconsider the idea. Just hearing it triggered an emotion that made him return to the current moment. He had had what he called a blow-away idea, an idea that is both so SIMPLE and yet so PROFOUND that at first it seems too simple to be so profound.

Many had asked whether God really needed 10 plagues to destroy the Egyptians, since one could easily have done it. Therefore they concluded that the sound-and-light show of plagues must have been to spiritually elevate the Jewish people and prepare them for redemption. Based on that, it occurred to him that the preparation was in order to so thoroughly rivet their attention on the present and instill them with hope that it would free them from the horrors of the past and despair in the future. The plagues, he realized, made the Jewish people mindful of the moment, and THAT led to their readiness for redemption.

He looked at his watch and saw that he was 10 minutes ahead of schedule. He calculated that he could explain the concept to his wife in that time, which would be a good review of his idea just before the class itself. To her surprise and delight, he poured some coffee from the pot, pulled up a chair, and began.

"It's like an atom. As you are probably aware," he began, talking as one expert to another, "an atom is the smallest unit of ordinary matter that constitutes a chemical element. Every solid, liquid, gas, and plasma is composed of neutral or ionized atoms. Atoms are extremely small: typical sizes are around 100 picometers, 10^{-10} mm, a ten-millionth of a millimeter, or 1/254,000,000 of an inch, if I recall my grade-eleven physics."

"Of course I know that," she said, pretending to be serious.

"And yet…if you blow up some atoms in a nuclear explosion, the result is a release of devastating energy many times greater than the size of the atoms involved in it!"

"And therefore?" she asked, not sure of the point he was making.

"And therefore," he continued, "it is amazing how much power and energy exist everywhere at all times, but to which we average people are completely oblivious."

"True."

"But not the nuclear physicists. They are not only aware of the energy surrounding them in every atom that makes up their reality, but they are even aware of how to access and harness it. It's an AWESOME power that can lay waste to an entire city, or power countless others. If I'm not mistaken, part of our electric grid is nuclear power."

"All very fascinating, but—"

"But we will have to continue this discussion later on," he said, checking his watch again, surprised at how quickly the 10 minutes went by. "Time sure flies when you talk nuclear physics," he added, using humor to soften the blow of an abrupt ending.

"I suppose so," she said, not hiding her disappointment.

Leaving his coffee half finished, he quickly got up just as the taxi out front honked, justifying his hurried exit.

"Tonight, b'ezras Hashem," he said grabbing his computer bag and an oblong carton while heading for the door, "right after the children go to sleep."

They said their goodbyes quickly, as she wondered which one would forget to bring up the discussion again many hours later.

The outdoor gathering was much larger than previous sessions. "I'm sorry I didn't sign up earlier, but..." he heard from several new people who were more than happy to pay extra just to attend for that one day. "Put the word 'redemption' in a title," he would later tell his wife, "and people come out from all over."

"Imagine if redemption, which we have awaited for thousands of years now, were not something that we ourself have to CREATE...as we tend to think. And because we tend to think like this, we tend to despair when we are not successful at CREATING it...or that events which seem to be leading to redemption don't RESULT in redemption. And here we are, thousands of years later, still waiting for the FINAL redemption, completely unsure about when GOD might bring it."

Redemption is ALWAYS a fascinating topic, but this point about it was SUPER fascinating. It's like someone telling you that you're not so mild-mannered after all, because you possess tremendous amounts of latent energies and powers that you just haven't tapped into yet. It's SO empowering, and therefore SO exciting.

"Redemption is in the air," Yirmi continued to the undivided attention of 60-plus people, apparently including some rabbanim and professionals. "And I don't just mean because of where we're holding historically right now. I mean it is LITERALLY in the AIR… in every atom and molecule that makes up the world in which we live. It has ALWAYS been in the air, ever since Creation itself."

Some people were so intrigued by and excited about the idea that they chose to stand at the back of the group instead of sitting on either chairs or benches.

"So why are we still in exile?" he asked the large gathering, many of whom probably knew the answer but figured that they weren't actually being asked for their input, at least not yet.

"The answer is basic, though tragic…" he said as his voice trailed off, expressing his sadness. "It's because we just haven't realized that it was there…in the air…or known how to access it…even though we have on occasion done so, usually accidentally."

"For thousands of years mankind has been surrounded by atoms, totally unaware of what they were or how much energy they possessed. Even once they were discovered, it was more by hypothesis than proven fact. Atoms are so extremely small that it's impossible to view them with a light microscope. The best we have been able to do is develop a number of techniques to observe and study their structure.

"But that in itself was enough to unleash the fury of an atomic bomb…or to harness atomic energy to light up our cities."

He paused and looked out in the distance. As he did, he reflected, "We may not understand the Kabbalah behind a moment of Creation…how every moment of time is a permutation of a Name of God…but we know enough to be able to tap into the awesome redemption energy it possesses—not to CREATE redemption but rather to RELEASE it on Creation."

He paused to give people an opportunity to digest the idea, and during that moment the soft rustling of a gentle breeze could be heard in the background, adding to the drama of the place…AND the moment.

"I would ask that all of you stand up so I can show you a little of what I mean."

After sitting for 30 minutes, some struggled to get up, making others who stood at the periphery somewhat grateful that they had remained standing the whole time.

"Nice view," he said casually, as people got to their feet. It truly was, just one of many all over Eretz

Yisroel. The mountains were not the highest nor the valleys the deepest. The lakes were smaller than in most places and the forests weren't nearly as robust as others around the world. But it didn't matter. The biblical history of the Jewish people that oozed out of it all and the presence of the Shechinah that pervaded even every blade of grass MORE than made up for it.

He let people take in the amazing view, which would hopefully encourage them to slip into a kind of meditative state. Then, pointing off into the distance, he asked, "Can everyone see that beautiful little sitting area over there?"

First they looked at his arm to see where he was pointing, and then they looked to see what he was pointing at. The suggestion that they should be able to see something worth looking at made them try hard.

Finally he said, "Of course you can't see it. If you could, you'd have far better vision than anyone else. That's why you will find some binoculars in the box on the table for your viewing pleasure…Please use them, and then pass them around since we have more people than binoculars."

By the oohing and aahing he could tell that people found what he wanted them to see, a beautifully landscaped sitting area nestled among mature trees that overlooked it like loving parents.

"Hey, wait," a voice said, "someone is waving to

me!"

"That's not possible!" another responded, taking the binoculars to see for himself. "If we can't see someone, he certainly can't see—"

He stopped mid-sentence, because it certainly looked as if the older man were in fact looking and waving right at him!

"How is that possible?" he said in a softer tone, as other people corroborated the mystery.

Yirmi just smiled, enjoying the moment. Then he checked his watch and decided it was time to make his point.

"It's possible," Yirmi said, "because..." he paused as everyone turned to hear his explanation, "I arranged with that gentleman to wave in this direction at exactly 2:15 p.m. He couldn't really see you...but acted as if he could."

Although the ruse elicited some smiles, everyone wondered about the connection of the stunt to what they had been learning.

"You're probably wondering what the point of all this is."

Heads nodded in agreement.

"I wanted to show you how you can look right at something, think you see all there is to see, and yet with enhanced vision see much more that was there the entire time...something that literally changes your mind about what you were looking at, and maybe even the way you live.

"I remember once being in an office when someone came in and said that the police had just towed away a car. No one paid much attention. Then the person went on to describe the car, and all of a sudden someone came to life! He became upset and animated…grabbed his coat and ran out the door."

"People felt a combination of humor and sympathy. But I also felt some awe. I thought, 'Wow…he was like a human bomb that just blew up. He went from LOW to HIGH energy in a matter of seconds. Just imagine what my life would be like if I could do THAT every moment!'

"Okay, not EVERY moment, because that would burn me out. But certainly more moments than I do now. So much of our life just seems to slip by, like an expert thief working undetected."

He paused, then reached out as if quickly grabbing a passing fly, at the same time saying, "This moment has redemption potential in it!" He made the same movement again as he said, "And THIS moment has redemption potential!"

Then looking at everyone in front of him, he said, "You want to know how I know?"

Heads automatically nodded yes.

"Because according to Torah, history can only be in one of two modes, exile OR redemption. There isn't any other possibility from a Torah perspective, even if it seems as if there is…and has been over the last while. If the Jewish people are not in exile but deserve to be, then history will inch its way in that direction until it finally happens, as it did after the destruction of the First Temple and every other time the Jewish people lost their independence.

"But if the Jewish people are already IN exile, then history changes direction and moves immediately in the direction of redemption…even if it looks otherwise. How much more so when we are still being exiled from one country to another and suffering terrible antisemitism along the way."

"This is essentially what God told Moshe when he complained about the increased severity of the slavery at the end of *Parashas Shemos*. Moshe said, 'You call increased hardship of slavery redemption?' God answered him, 'You're watching redemption take place before your very eyes, and you complain?' And the rest of us say, 'Huh?' as we identify with MOSHE'S point of view.

"Furthermore, let us not forget that Moshe Rabbeinu had been on the earth for 79 years before God tapped him for the job of redeemer. THAT'S SEVENTY-NINE YEARS! And while he was getting on-the-job training to become the future leader of God's people, exile deepened for that people…an unusual mix of exile and redemption at the same time."

More heads nodding in agreement.

"But it was really all for the sake of redemption…because THAT was where history was going."

He sighed deeply.

"The Second Temple was destroyed almost 2,000 years ago. We lost our independence even before then…and in fact Kristallnacht in 1938 was literally the 2,000th year after we did…when Pompey took control of Israel in 63 BCE. TWO THOUSAND YEARS OF GOLUS EDOM!

"And now, according to many calculations, at the end of THIS period of history, Moshiach has to be close…HAS TO BE. I could spend the next hour explaining that, as well as the other amazing events of the last 70 years that support the idea that despite all the setbacks and close calls, we ARE in GEULAH-MODE!"

He must have made some impression, because he could feel the energy of excitement as he spoke. Even the hard-sells were either smiling in agreement or at least holding their peace. One thing was for sure: the moment was beginning to burst with a sense of redemption, and he himself was being uplifted by it.

"WE may not be working toward redemption, but GOD sure is. And you can see it…if you become MINDFUL of what has happened—and often SO miraculously—over the last 70 to 80 years. Even NEGATIVE events can now be viewed in terms of how they helped the geulah process.

"Although I could also spend an additional hour on why God works that way in the first place, instead you might like to check out some of the books by Rabbi Pinchas Winston on the subject. They are based on many important mainstream sources, and I found the information invaluable.

"The main thing for our discussion now is that if God is moving history in the direction of redemption, and there is NO reason to assume otherwise, then it means that so much opportunity to help with that process…either physically OR spiritually…must exist… EVERY moment…if we just pay attention to what is going on, what is available, and what we can do.

"And here's the truly important part. Once God sees that people are on the same historic page as He is…that they are REAL with the concept of redemption, then He helps them out. He directs them…opens their eyes to things they never saw before…gets the proper books to them…makes the proper connections for them. I think you get the idea. As they say, if you mind the moment, then the moment minds you."

"Where?" a lone voice called out.

"Excuse me?"

"Where does it say that?" the voice continued, now easily traceable. "I like the way that sounds."

"It's a gemora," Yirmi answered, "the last daf of *Brochos*."

Yirmi could see that, as simple as the question

was, the person asking it was a person of learning. So he spoke more in yeshivishe terms.

"*Samech-Dalet, amud alef…64a.* That's where the Talmud says that for 'anyone who tries to push off the moment,' meaning that he tries to accomplish something that is clearly not appropriate at the moment, 'the moment will push him off'—that is, his effort will backfire. But, the Talmud continues, if the person allows himself to be pushed off by the moment, meaning that he waits for a more appropriate time to say or do what he wants, then the moment will be pushed off for him—in other words, the time will come for him to be successful. That," Yirmi concluded, "tells us the importance of minding the moments of our life, and the positive consequences of doing so.

"But it is not the MAIN point, which I want to reiterate. This is. Contrary to conventional wisdom, redemption is not something that you create. It is the AUTOMATIC result of an internal process that we all must go through to first achieve personal redemption—and that, believe it or not—was the reason for the 10 plagues in Egypt.

"After all, if the goal were to weaken or destroy the Egyptians, one plague would have been enough. According to many, such as the Leshem Shevo V'Achlamah and the Pri Tzaddik, the plagues were primarily for the Jewish people, to transform them into people who could GO into freedom. Each plague was like a dose of spiritual medicine to strengthen and transform the slave nation on its way to becoming a Torah nation."

"How did that work? Each plague increased the dosage of God revelation, expanding the nation's ability to grasp the reality of God in everyday life. Over the course of 116 years of slavery, the Egyptians had done everything they could to drain the Jewish people of all godliness. They almost succeeded. We're told that if Moshe Rabbeinu had not gone down to Egypt when he did, 190 years EARLY, the Jewish people would have become spiritually irredeemable.

"Once he did show up on the job and began speaking in God's Name and doing His wonders, the Jewish people were reintroduced to the God of their fathers, and more importantly, to the God of their history.

"In plague after plague God revealed Himself more and more. He Himself carried out the tenth and final plague, the death of the firstborn. His reality became so clear that free will itself was temporarily suspended, and a broken and humbled Pharaoh had no choice but to free the Jews previously under his control."

"You'll notice that when it finally came time to leave Egypt, the Jewish people did not have to fight anyone. They simply walked out, just like that, as if they had been free people the entire time!

"What had changed," he further explained, "was the STATE OF MIND of the Jewish people. As they became more God-oriented, they became freer, and this is why.

"People tend to live in the past or the future. The present is just a threshold over which the former passes on its way to becoming the latter. Quite simply, being subject to time—meaning we can't control its flow—we have to deal with its constant change. It's like standing stationary in front of a conveyer belt as your luggage continues to move closer to you, and then past you.

"Just the opposite is true for God. He is NOT subject to time, being ABOVE or BEYOND it. Nothing changes for HIM, even if it seems to change for US. He is ETERNAL, and therefore there is no past or future for Him, only the present.

"Most interesting is that if you tap into God, in whatever capacity He allows you to, you essentially tap into the only REAL version of the present. You tap into the only REAL portal to eternity. Shabbos, as the Talmud says, is one-sixtieth of the World-to-Come because there is more GOD in Shabbos, at least more of Him to sense, than in the six working days of the week.

"That is why Torah is a portal to the moment. Mitzvos attach a person to God. Learning Torah attaches us to God. Both attach us to the only real source of 'present' there is, God Himself. Redemption does not exist in the past and it certainly does not exist in the future. It exists only in the PRESENT, and that's what the 10 plagues ultimately did for the Jewish people—they brought the nation closer to God, closer to the present, closer to freedom. As the mishnah says, 'Freedom was engraved on the tablets.'"

He paused for a long moment, looked around at the crowd, glanced at his watch, took a deep breath, and finally said, "Let me conclude this series of classes and the program by saying that being mindful of a moment means being mindful of God IN the moment. When people make a point of minding the moment, and MINING the moment for its potential, they are in fact getting in touch with God. They may not think so or feel it directly, but that is what is going on.

"And if you know that is what is actually going on, and you make a point of knowing it from the start, then think about how much further ahead you will be in the redemption department, even as others around you still struggle with exile. It's a whole different plane of existence, a whole different plan for life."

He stopped talking, and the place was absolutely quiet. He couldn't have orchestrated it better, and he thanked God to himself. He quickly thought over the material to see if there were anything he needed to add, but felt that by this point, less was really more.

He thanked everyone for coming to the course, and God for allowing him to give it. He took a few questions and decided that, because of the lack of time, he would make himself available for a question-and-answer session the following week. Everyone seemed fine with that, and they made their way to the various forms of transportation they had used to get there.

Yirmi looked around to make sure nothing was left behind. Then he looked out into the distance one last time, and to his surprise he thought he could see the man waving at him again. He squinted, while realizing that without retrieving a pair of binoculars, it was impossible to see that far.

"Hmm," he said to himself, somewhat suspicious. Then he decided that it didn't matter whether he truly saw what he thought he saw or it was just an illusion. It still made him intensely aware of the moment, and that WAS real. He felt a surging desire within to thank God. He felt SO connected…and so FREE.

THE FOLLOWING TITLES are all the books written over the years. Some books may no longer be in print, but many are still available in either PDF or Kindle formats. Visit the Thirtysix.org OnLine Bookstore, or Amazon for more information, or to order online.

The Unbroken Chain of Jewish Tradition, 1985
The Eternal Link, 1990
If Only I Were Wealthy, 1992
If Only I Understood Why, 1993
If Only I Could See the Forest, 1993
If Only I Could Stay, 1993
If Only Great Was Greater, 1993

The Y Factor, 1994
Life's a Thrill, 1994
No Atheists in a Foxhole, 1994
Changes that Last Forever, 1994
The Making of a Great Jewish Leader, 1994
Bereishis: A Beginning with No End, 1994
The Wonderful World of Thirtysix, 1995
Redemption to Redemption, 1997
The Big Picture, 1998
Perceptions, 1998
Not Just Another Scenario, 2001
At the Threshold, 2001
Anticipating Redemption, 2002
Sha'ar HaGilgulim, 2002
Hadran (Hebrew), 2004
Talking About the End-of-Days, 2005
Talking About Eretz Yisroel, 2005
The Physics of Kabbalah, 2006
Be Positive, 2007
Geulah b'Rachamim, 2007
God.calm, 2007
Just Passing Through, 2007
On the Same Page, 2007
The Equation of Life, 2007
No Such Victim, 2009
Survival in 10 Easy Steps, 2009
Not Just Another Scenario 2, 2011
All In Your Mind, 2011

The Light of Thirtysix, 2011
The Last Exile, 2011
Drowning in Pshat, 2012
Drown No More, 2012
Shas Man, 2013
The Mystery of Jewish History, 2013
Survival Guide For the End-of-Days, 2013
Deeper Perceptions, 2013
Chanukah Lite, 2015
The Hitchhiker's Guide to Armageddon, 2016
Purim Lite, 2016
Pesach Lite, 2016
The Torah Empowerment Seminar, 2016
Siman Tov (Hebrew), 2016
The Fabric of Reality, 2016
Addendum, 2016
Fundamentals of Reincarnation, 2017
Reincarnation Clarified, 2016
All About Energy, 2017
What Goes Around, 2017
The God Experience, 2017
What in Heaven, 2017
The God Experience, Part 2, 2017
The God Experience, Part 3, 2017
It's About Time, 2017
Need to Know, 2017
Perceptions, Volume 2, 2017
Once Revealed, Twice Concealed, 2017

The Art of Chayn, 2017
A Matter of Laugh or Death, 2018
Geulah b'Rachamim Program, V. 1, 2018
Geulah b'Rachamim Program, V. 2, 2018
Geulah b'Rachamim Program, V. 3, 2018
Point of Acceptance, 2018
See Ya, 2018
In Discussion: Bereishis, 2018
Reincarnation Again, 2018
A Separate Matter, 2018
In Discussion: Shemos, 2019
A Search for Self, 2019
A Search for Trust, 2019
In Discussion: Bamidbar, 2019
How It Might Play Out, 2019
In Discussion: Vayikra, 2019
Where Are My Emotions Now, 2019
In Discussion: Devarim, 2019
The Early Years, 2019
Oh, So Blind, 2019
Not So Bad? 2019
Sha'ar HaPesukim: Shemos, 2019
The Fix, 2020
Sha'ar HaPesukim: Bereishis, 2020
Preparing for Redemption, 2020
Mindfulness, Torah & Redemption, 2020

For more information, write to pinchasw@thirtysix.org.

a **4-part webinar** covering
many of the ideas in the book,
and going beyond it.

Available through the thirtysix.org
online store.

thirtysix.org